Thomas Prior

His Life, Times and Legacy

By
Teddy Fennelly

Arderin Publishing Company

Thomas Prior – His Life, Times and Legacy

First Published 2001
by
Arderin Publishing Company
in conjunction with
The Leinster Express,
Dublin Road,
Portlaoise,
County Laois
Republic of Ireland.

ISBN 0-86335-041-0

Designed and Printed by Leinster Leader Ltd., Naas, Co. Kildare.

Contents

Acknowledgements

President, executive and staff of the RDS for their cooperation and for allowing access to archives, memorabilia and printed material

Mary Kelleher, Librarian, RDS, for her encouragement, guidance and patience, whose invaluable help made this publication possible

Matt Dempsey, Chairman of RDS Management Committee, for his advice and support

Gerry Maher, Co. Librarian, and staff Laois Co. Library, particularly Cáit Kavanagh, Paddy Macken and Patricia Lynch

National Library of Ireland

Trinity College Library, Dublin

Dr. Máire Kennedy, The Gilbert Library, Dublin

Laois Heritage Society

John Colclough of Country House Tours and Irish Incentives Ltd. (website: tourismresources.ie) (e.mail: cht@indigo.ie) for information supplied on ancestry and family of Thomas Prior

The Reverend Sean O'Doherty, P.P., Durrow, Co. Laois

Imelda Kehoe, Gowran, Co. Kilkenny

Rev. John Murray, Archdeacon of Cashel and Ossory

Paul Ryan, Rathdowney

Henry Arthur and Mrs. Dunne, the Garrison, Rathdowney

Desmond Townshend, Bagenalstown, Co. Carlow

Fergus Mulligan, Ranelagh

Special thanks to my son, David, for his guidance and wisdom in preparing and presenting the book

Last, but not least, to my wife, Carmel, and family for their patience and support

Foreword

On the 250th anniversary of Thomas Prior's death I welcome this biography by Teddy Fennelly. It is a timely publication which I hope will bring awareness of the life and achievements of this great man to many more people. The book is set against the background of the turbulent history of early eighteenth century Ireland, recovering from the wars of the previous century. It sheds light on Prior's upbringing in Rathdowney, his education in Kilkenny and at Trinity College Dublin.

It has often been said that Thomas Prior was the prime force behind the founding of the Royal Dublin Society in 1731, or as it was then, the Dublin Society. The principles he advocated of voluntary service for the public good and the development of ideas and enterprises to benefit the whole country are still held today by his successors. One of Prior's greatest attributes was his ability to stimulate others to provide practical solutions for the social and economic problems facing Irish society at the time. The initiatives taken then have evolved over the centuries to become some of Ireland's greatest institutions of culture, learning and agriculture.

Thomas Prior was a man of great moral courage and social conscience. Unusual for his time, he was prepared to be critical of the Establishment of the day. A particular example was the publication of his lists of absentee landlords whose neglect and greed drained the country's resources and caused severe economic hardship. He also sought to reform the repressive laws of the previous century.

We at the RDS strive to keep Prior's memory alive and are currently involved in the refurbishment of his memorial. Originally erected in Christ Church Cathedral in 1756, the memorial was formerly restored by the Society in 1891. His spirit, which this book captures so well, should be a stimulus to RDS members today. We must continue the work he started, identifying the needs and problems within Irish society, and finding innovative ways in overcoming them. We will then be making a positive contribution to the welfare of the whole country.

Col W. A. Ringrose,
President, RDS

Introduction

Thomas Prior was the inspiration and driving force behind the foundation of the Dublin Society, which was to become the Royal Dublin Society in 1820. Established in 1731 with the aim of improving the social and economic life of the country, it developed better farming methods, set up new industries and gave a platform and support to the promotion of science and the arts.

From that tiny seed sown by Prior and his associates grew a national institution that would become an enriching influence on almost every aspect of Irish life over the decades and centuries to come. The Society was the catalyst from which sprang many other worthy national institutions.

To fully appreciate his legacy, Prior and his achievements must be set in the context of his time, circumstance and place. His grandfather was an English army captain who had been granted a large estate in Rathdowney in the Queen's County (now County Laois) and Barony of Ossory which was confiscated from "Irish Papists" following the Cromwellian conquest in the mid-1600s. His father was a colonel in the militia who served on the Williamite side during the Jacobite War some forty years later. These campaigns finally brought the whole of Ireland under the control of England. The conquest was complete. With their natural leaders either killed or in exile, the spirit of the Irish had finally been crushed.

The Catholic Irish who survived the campaigns of genocide of the 17th century had been reduced to a state of utter despair and destitution, scavenging the land for the scraps that fell from the masters' tables. The ruthless imposition of the Penal Code, which effectively denied them of every basic human right, had compounded their state of slavery. As the century turned, they posed no threat whatsoever to the Anglo-Irish establishment and would remain an impotent force for the best part of the eighteenth century.

The new ascendancy viewed the situation from a different perspective, however. The horrors of recent wars had left many scars and the young Anglo-Irish grew up, as their fathers and grandfathers had done before them, seeing and believing the old Irish as their arch-enemies, craving an opportunity for vengeance. Although they were now firmly in possession of almost all the best land and resources as well as having military support, the settlers, thinly scattered throughout the country, continued to feel vulnerable.

In the midst of the naked oppression perpetrated by the colonists, fuelled by the foundless fears which drove them to even further extremes of tyranny, a ray of light, which had its origins on the continent, began to pierce the darkness of 17th and early 18th century Ireland. The Age of Enlightenment had dawned. Already in England, the Royal Society was drawing together the genius of the age; Isaac Newton, Robert Boyle and John Locke were some of its most prominent members. It was at Kilkenny School that the young Thomas Prior first fell under the spell of this new enlightenment. Having received a rounded education at Kilkenny, he later studied at Trinity College, Dublin and Oxford University which gave him a good knowledge of the classics, literature and economics. It was in these institutions that his liberal ideology was formed and that he developed friendships with the brilliant philosopher, George Berkeley, and other gifted academics. Their collective intellectual output, liberal attitudes and practical achievements would have a significant influence for good on the Irish economy and society in the years ahead.

The colonists, tenuous settlers in a ravaged land, looked to their mother country for the increased military security they felt was needed. England gave them that backing, but at a price, exacted in economic restrictions and political subservience. As far as the Westminster Parliament was concerned, England's economic welfare had to be protected at all costs. This policy led to the stagnation of the Irish economy during the opening half of the eighteenth century. The more privileged were far from happy to see their incomes levelling off but it was the poor who suffered most. Famine stalked the land, adding to the absolute distress of the native Irish. If the Old Irish were stateless and denied all civil and religious rights by the Protestant ascendancy, the Anglo-Irish found in turn that they were second class citizens as far as the London establishment were concerned. They resented such treatment. The desire for greater autonomy led to a growing nationalist movement, not in this instance in the wider Irish context but rather the creation of a new nation for the ruling minority.

As early as 1698, William Molyneux published a pamphlet putting forward the ascendancy claim. His *Case for Ireland Stated* outlined Anglo-Irish concerns and strongly argued against the English veto on decisions made by the Irish Parliament. Lord Molesworth made a less political but more practical contribution in his pamphlet entitled *Some*

Considerations for Promoting Agriculture and Employing the Poor, which appeared in 1723. He identified the middlemen as the ruination of farms and farmers alike and urged a change in the law both for landlord and tenant.

Jonathan Swift, one of the greatest satirists in world literature, used his biting invective to undermine London's authority. In *The Drapier Letters*, he foiled English plans to introduce debased coinage, known as "Wood's halfpence", into Ireland in an effort to address the problem of the shortage of small coin.

With the publication in 1729 of *A Modest Proposal*, a grotesque satire based on the twin Irish problems of overpopulation and food shortage, Swift soon became the darling of the Irish ascendancy.

Prior was equally concerned about Ireland's ills. Without the venom of Swift, he put forward a well reasoned plan for the improvement of the deplorable economic condition of the country. In his *Observations on Coin* of 1729, Prior used the weight of economic argument rather than piercing invective in addressing the problem.

In the same year, Prior published an even more important and controversial pamphlet. His *List of Absentees* was a landmark publication and showed his extraordinary courage. He named those landlords who spent most of their time abroad, drawing incomes from Ireland but putting little back into the country's economy. Prior estimated that a sum of more than £600,000 was being sent out of the country each year, which was a huge drain on its limited resources. He concluded with a damning indictment of the disregard for the conditions in which the poor were forced to live.

Prior decided to take his plan of action a stage further, however. Enough had been written on the subject of the Irish economy. The time had now come to act. He floated his ideas among like-minded public-spirited men in the Dublin professional world, where he was well-known and respected. While others decried England's policies on Irish economic affairs, Prior was convinced that Ireland could do much for herself by encouraging new industries and more productive methods of farming. On 25th June 1731, fourteen men met in the rooms of the Philosophical Society in Trinity College and agreed to form a society with a view to these ends. Prior would now devote his time and energy to driving the aims of the new organisation, named the Dublin Society, until his death twenty years later.

Prior's health failed in the winter of 1750/'51. As he lay on his death-bed, his close associates in the Dublin Society must have figured greatly in his reflections; men like William Maple, long-time curator and registrar; Arthur Dobbs, who had called for an improved system of tenure for the Irish peasant and who had gone in search of the North-West Passage; Rev. Samuel Madden, better known as "Premium" Madden, and all the other dear colleagues who had helped establish and copper-fasten the future of the Society. His thoughts would have surely cast back to his friendship with Chesterfield, the benevolent viceroy who gave Prior and the Society his full and unequivocal support. So too with Bartholomew Mosse who, when he sought backing to improve the appalling conditions of poor expectant mothers, found Prior a friend in his time of need. The result was the founding of the Rotunda Hospital, the first hospital of its kind in the western world. Then there was Berkeley, his oldest and most trusted friend. The two men's constant exchange of ideas had had a profound influence on him and his activities throughout his life.

Thomas Prior was a remarkable man. Although the ascendancy class to which he belonged often behaved disgracefully in their role as rulers of a new Ireland, Prior rose above the ruthlessness, blindness and bitterness of the throng of his contemporaries to establish himself as a true patriot, a man who put his country and the welfare of its people – all its people – before his own self-interest. There were few of his era who could surpass his intellect, sincerity and courage and none who could match his compassion and his legacy of practical achievement.

Prior closed his eyes on this world on 21st October, 1751, in Garrison House, Rathdowney, the same house, perhaps even the same room, in which he had first seen the light of day some seventy years earlier. A memorial stands in the parish church which still services the local Church of Ireland community. The exact location of his final resting place in the old graveyard nearby is now unknown; a strange and perhaps telling twist of fate for a man so modest in life. Another memorial, erected by the Society he founded, is located in the south porch of Christchurch Cathedral, in recognition of his lifelong work for the city of Dublin and for Ireland. Berkeley wrote the inscription for the memorial – a fitting tribute indeed. It was, however, the blossoming and the prospering of the Royal Dublin Society that would remain his greatest lasting tribute.

CHAPTER 1

Family Background

Thomas Prior's father and grandfather were also named Thomas and both were army officers, one in the regular army and the other in the County Militia. His grandfather, Captain Thomas Prior, first came to Ireland with his regiment in 1636 and, apparently, served in the campaigns against the Catholic Confederate army because he was the beneficiary of land confiscated by the Cromwellians from the Irish at the conclusion of the war.[1] Carrigan informs us that, in 1653, "Rathdowney was forfeited by Morgan Cashin and Bryan McWilliam Fitzpatrick, Irish papists, and granted with portions of Ballyhenry or Harristown, Ballybuggy and Kilcoran to Captain Thomas Prior."[2] Carrigan also notes that on 8 February 1642 "Barnaby or Bryan McWilliam Fitzpatrick of 'Raghdowny' was outlawed by proclamation of the Lord Justices, for taking part in the great National Uprising of the previous year. He was afterwards Captain in the Confederate army, and was one of the last to lay down his arms in 1652. One of his sons was slain before Borris-in-Ossory, in 1642". A Morgan Cashin also died in the same battle.[3]

The Fitzpatricks (MacGiolla Phadraig) were the old Gaelic lords of North Ossory. Different branches of the clan owned huge tracts of land and Fitzpatrick castles dominated the landscape of the region. As with the vast majority of Catholics, most of the Fitzpatrick estates were forfeited under the various 16th and 17th century confiscations. The Cashins were an old Gaelic clan in the area and had also fought on the Catholic side during the long and bloody war which ended in the eventual rout at the hands of Cromwell. The family names of Fitzpatrick, Cashin and, to a lesser extent, Prior, still survive in the south-west region (Upper Ossory) of Laois today.

In September 1653 the war was officially declared at an end and to the victors the spoils. Under the Act of Satisfaction the counties of Waterford, Limerick, Tipperary, Meath, Westmeath, Armagh, Down, Louth, King's County and Queen's County were to answer all claims of adventurers and arrears of the army since 5 June 1649. The Second Court of Claims under the Act of Settlement opened on 4 January 1666 and some eight hundred acres of the confiscated land in the neighbourhood of Rathdowney were certified in the name of Thomas Pryor on 7 September in the same year. The total area is identified in the Petty Survey.

Captain Prior owned an estate at Ely in Cambridgeshire. Coincidentally Oliver Cromwell was left property by an uncle in 1638 at Ely and sat for Cambridge during the Short Parliament of 1640 and during the Long Parliament in which he was a vehement supporter of Puritanism.[4] Apart from this geographical detail and the army connection, there is no record of Prior having any close or personal association with the infamous Lord-Lieutenant.

Captain Prior had three children, Thomas and Richard and a daughter, Mary. Richard was outlawed under the Act of Attainder of the Irish Parliament of James II and forfeited his share of the Irish estate. His name appeared on a list of more than two thousand landowners who were to be attainted of high treason, unless they could prove their innocence by personal appearance before the appointed day. These were all people who had fled their homes for fear of their lives. There were forty-five landowners named from the Queen's County.[5] Richard fled to England where he looked after his family's business interests there, which he inherited on his father's death in 1691. He continued to live on the family estate in Cambridge until his death in 1726.

The Irish estate passed to the Captain Prior's eldest son, Thomas, who rose to the rank of colonel in the Queen's County Militia. Unlike his brother, Colonel Prior risked staying on at Rathdowney during the days of the Jacobite Parliament and his name was not included on the list of those outlawed. After the Battle of the Boyne and the hasty retreat and flight to France of James II, most of the country came under the control of King William's forces. The demoralised Catholics were left at the mercy of the rampaging Williamites – and mercy was in short supply. The rebels behind enemy lines hit back with a campaign of guerilla warfare. Queen's County was well behind the Williamite lines and was used as an area of quarter. The remnants of the Catholic resistance in the county had taken refuge in the bogs and mountains, particularly in the wild fastness of the Slieve Blooms, from where they moved out to murder stragglers, steal horses, attack convoys and interfere with the post and communications. It was a spontaneous uprising of ordinary people reacting to the dire treatment being meted out to them by mostly foreign soldiers. To some extent it was orchestrated by the Irish army across the Shannon in order to harass the Williamites and to disrupt their movements. The guerillas became known in folklore as the Raparees, a term which comes from the name for a small pike they used carry stuffed under their shirts. To the Williamites they were outlaws but in rebel Catholic, and later in republican and nationalist folklore, they were renowned in song and story as heroic and chivalrous champions of the oppressed native Irish.

Casualties were incurred on both sides as a result of their lightning attacks on Williamite camps and patrols. Protestants landowners were pressurised by the military into countering the menace and formed into local voluntary forces to bring the guerillas to heel. In Queen's County a local Militia was formed in early 1691, which consisted of 500 men and 50 horse, to deal with the raparees. Captain Tom Prior (later Colonel), because he had not fled the country on James' brief triumphant return, was now looked on by his peers for leadership among the county's Protestant community. He was appointed a Commissioner in the Militia, which was presided over by Major Cornelius Woods. The Raparees were fearless and just as ruthless as their pursuers. When apprehended the outlaws were dealt with summarily. Samples of the Militia's dispensation of instant justice can be found among the news items noted for Queen's County in the "Dublin Intelligence", a contemporary Williamite propaganda newspaper. In one dated February 1691, it was reported that "several raparees were killed and hanged by the militia near Mountrath". Another item informs that Major Weldon was in charge of a successful operation against raparees in Mountmellick and that seventy were killed in the Ballybrittas area by a Militia party led by Major Woods.

But the Queen's County Militia also offered the olive branch to the rebels. A letter was sent from Dublin instructing them to round up a number of the most dangerous Roman Catholics. Local opinion did not concur with the belief in Dublin that the names supplied were dangerous rebels, however, and instead of arresting those named the Militia commissioners circulated twenty or more "chiefs of the Irish ring" with letters offering them protection in return for cessation of raparee activity.

After the war more land confiscations followed. Extremely harsh religious laws were introduced against a Catholic population crushed by coercion, broken in spirit and deprived by law of every basic human right. Catholic clergy were forced to flee the country under penalty of death but many priests refused to desert their flock and paid the ultimate price. The local militia were empowered to enforce the penal code and to seek out and eliminate renegade clergymen. Canon O'Hanlon in his "History of the Queen's County" refers to an incident at the Prior home, Garrison House, "probably before 1700", in which priest-hunters were given a reward of £5 for the head of a murdered priest. (Appendix 3) This grisly visit by priest-hunters took place during the residency of

Colonel Prior at Garrison House. If O'Hanlon is factually correct, then it has to be assumed that the reward was paid by Colonel Prior although the account of the incident does not mention him by name. Nor do we know if his son, the teenage Thomas, was aware of the incident.

The outskirts of the cities and towns were filled with homeless paupers and beggars, mostly dispossessed, living in atrocious conditions. Their hovels were a breeding ground for disease, public disorder and criminal activities. Highwaymen and desperados roamed the countryside exacting booty and ransom from vulnerable travellers. Robberies were often accompanied by murder. Little is known of the exact circumstances but it was in a confrontation with outlaws that Colonel Prior was fatally wounded in 1700. The young Thomas Prior, then 19, was a student at Trinity College at the time and on the tragic death of his father he apparently took time out from his studies to be with his family in Rathdowney for an extended period that year.

Prior kept in touch with his interests in Rathdowney throughout his life but he grew away from most members of his family. He never married and with the exception of his aunt, Mary, in Rathdowney, and his uncle, Richard, in Cambridge, with whom he enjoyed a close mutual friendship, he had little contact with other family members. He was estranged from his early years from his brother, Richard, and half-brothers, Robert and William, as noted by Clarke "of whose riotous behaviour he disapproved".[6] This disapproval was underlined when he disinherited them in favour of his first cousin, John Murray (later Murray-Prior), only son of Mary and her husband Rev. Thomas Murray, to whom he left his estate.[7] Thomas Prior may have enjoyed less than a fulfilling family life but he developed a number of close and lasting friendships outside the family circle. His city residence was at Bolton Street where "two faithful servants, Pat Bryan and John Rourk attended to his needs".[8] This became the meeting place for his friends and it was with the help of such friends that he founded the Dublin Society in 1731.

References

(1) *Thomas Prior (1681-1751)* by Desmond Clarke. Dublin. 1951.

(2) *History and Antiquities of the Diocese of Ossory* by Rev. W. Carrigan. 1905. Desmond Clarke gives the year as 1655.

(3) *Some Account of the Ruinous Ecclesiastical Edifices, Forts, Castles, &c., with notes of Modern Events connected with the Queen's County and County of Kildare* by M. C. Carey. Maryborough. 1901. See Appendix 4.

(4) *The Cambridge Biographical Encyclopedia* edited by David Crystal (Cambridge Univ. Press. 1998. 2nd ed.).

(5) *History of the Queen's County* by J. Canon O'Hanlon and E. O'Leary. Dublin. 1914.

(6) As (2). See Appendix 1.

(7) Extract from *The General Armory of England, Scotland, Ireland and Wales* by Sir Bernard Burke. London. 1884. See Appendix 1.

(8) As (2).

CHAPTER 2

Enlightenment

Thomas Prior, the second son in his family, was ten years old when his grandfather, Captain Prior, died in 1691. His special industrious and intellectual qualities, which were so very evident in later life, must have been noted at an early age by his grandfather, who gives him a special mention in his will. The Jacobite revolt was brought to an end that year and he must have experienced the deep sense of relief felt by parents, siblings and the settler fraternity as a whole with the victory of the Protestant Williamites.

At the age of fifteen Prior was sent to Kilkenny for his educational grounding. Kilkenny School, also known as Kilkenny Grammar School, was founded in 1538 by Sir Piers Butler, 8th earl of Ormond, and his wife. James, 1st duke of Ormond, who was three times Lord Lieutenant, wrote the Charter which was signed in 1685 and it then became known as Kilkenny College. While it was a fee-paying institution, it was free to the children of those in Ormond's service and half-price to students from the city itself. It was regarded as the best educational establishment at the time in Ireland.

Among the many celebrities who were educated there was satirist and controversialist, Jonathan Swift (1667-1745), who was sent there in 1673. Prior was to strike up an acquaintance with Swift in later life and both shared broadly similar economic and social viewpoints though their means of expression differed greatly. Another famous writer, William Congreve (1670-1729), friend of Dryden, also began his education there, as did the Jesuit martyr, Edmund Campion, and historian, Richard Stanihurst (1547-1618), author of *De Rebus in Hibernia gestis Libri Quatuor* and friend of the Earl of Kildare over a century previously. These and other scholars from the Kilkenny school of learning must have had left a deep impression on the young Prior, but it was his contemporary, George Berkeley (1685-1753), who had a profound and lasting influence on him.

Though a few years his senior, Prior developed a close and lifelong friendship with Berkeley, who was later to become Bishop of Cloyne and one of the great philosophers of the 18th century. They corresponded with each other over many years. Prior kept Berkeley's letters and all are extant except for those of a three year period, from 1731 to 1734, which for some unknown reason are missing from the collection. It is from these letters that the many biographies on Berkeley are based and it is also from them that we can patch together an insight into the life and mindset of Prior, a very private and modest man, who left behind him precious little information of a personal nature despite his superb legacy of achievement in the public interest.

We know from Berkeley's writings that discipline was strict and the college rules harshly enforced at Kilkenny College. It was here they were first exposed to the classics, hebrew, poetry and oratory. Many of Prior's contemporaries are described as the sons of yeomen which was, as Clarke remarked, "a very typical English innovation". One of the students at the time was an Oliver Lodge who, like Prior, was a Queen's County boy. He later became Governor of Virginia, U.S.A. The well-known physicist and pioneer of radio-telegraphy, Sir Oliver Joseph Lodge, (1851-1940), was of the same family.[1] There were also sons of the local clergy, small gentry, attorneys and farmers on the rolls though later it went decidedly upmarket when "Kilkenny College began to be frequented by the scions of noble houses: the Desarts, Inchiquins, Morningtons, Charlemonts, Shandons and the rest".[2] The names on the school roll at the end of the seventeenth century have generally a 'new English' sound – as though dating from the Elizabethan, Cromwellian or Williamite plantations rather than from the Norman invasion; whereas the Ormonds, patrons of the College, were High Church or Tory with Cavalier and Norman-Irish associations.[3] The new settlers in Ireland had, however, tended to accept the Norman-Irish culture and leadership; moreover the settlements based on the confiscation of Roman Catholic land established some common interest between many of the old Norman-Irish and the newer settlers.[4] Kilkenny at the time was described as "the most pleasant and delightful town in the kingdom. Its complexion was not that of provincial mediocrity. The place was esteemed the most urbane in the kingdom, the most polite and well-bred".[5]

The College records for Prior are scant. The entry on his arrival there reads merely: "Pryor, Thomas. Aged 15. January 11, 1696-7." The only other entry refers to his time of leaving: "Mr. Prior left the second class, April 1699, and was entered in the University of Dublin." The urbane and cultured character of Kilkenny combined with the academic ambience and excellence of Kilkenny College must have had a profound and lasting impact on a highly intelligent and impressionable young man whose family background was puritan and militaristic and whose home was a settler's outpost surrounded by people regarded by the new English, to whose stock he belonged, as the "common enemy".[6] This was the Age of Enlightenment, a European intellectual movement influenced by the thinking of philosophers and scientists and having at its core a belief in reason as the key to human knowledge and progress, a sense of religious tolerance and a distrust of superstition. Prior had received a taste of enlightenment at Kilkenny which was to be further nurtured during his years at Trinity College.

At Trinity College he, along with Berkeley, Dobbs, Madden, Synge and others, came under the spell of the new thinking emanating from the Royal Society and a spirit of liberalism as expressed by the French philosopher, René Descartes (1596-1650), Englishman, John Locke (1632-1704) and the mathematician and physicist, Sir Isaac Newton (1642-1727). The death of his father in 1700 disrupted Prior's studies but he resumed his studies in 1701 when he was elected a Scholar of Trinity College and two years later he graduated as a Bachelor of Arts.

Ireland was still recovering from the effects of the Jacobite revolt as the century turned. Calm was now restored not so much by the balming clauses written into the Treaty of Limerick to soothe Catholic fears as by the non-compliance of the ruling establishment to these very clauses. Catholic rights, enshrined in the Treaty, were to be in line with those enjoyed by them following the Restoration of Charles II in 1660. This had been a period of greater religious tolerance than at any time since the Reformation. Instead of protecting Catholic rights, however, a series of penal restrictions were introduced by the new ascendancy in the decades that followed the signing of the Treaty. These enactments took away from Catholics one basic right after another. The absolute denial of land, religion, education and political or job opportunities to Catholics was seen as providing a means of security for the settlers and the ruling class. England supported these extreme measures brought in by the Irish Parliament. In the words of Burke, "It was a complete system, full of coherence, well digested and well composed in all its parts. It was a machine of wise and elaborate contrivance, as well fitted for the oppression, impoverishment, and degradation of a people, and the debasement of them in human nature itself, as ever proceeded from the perverted ingenuity of man."

These laws extracted everything that was left from the Catholic Irish. They were a spent force and would remain as such for the greater part of the eighteenth century. The new ascendancy did not feel all that secure, however. They knew that hatred burned with a passion in the hearts of the dispossessed Irish. They knew that the Protestant settlers were very much in the minority and were thinly scattered among a hostile population. They knew that the Catholics had been subdued many times previously but had always bounced back with a vengeance. Fears of a Catholic backlash, probably aided and abetted by sympathisers on the continent, persisted among the new English until well into the eighteenth century. They looked to England to provide their security which was duly provided, but at a price.

The Irish economy, still reeling from the effects of the recent war, was now further impeded by the exclusion of three-quarters of the population from participating in any form of industry or wealth creation. But it was the naked self-interest of the English that shook the Irish economy to its foundations and the outflow of money in rents and emoluments to people living abroad aggravated the situation. The growth of trade had helped create a powerful commercial class in England which exerted great political clout. They were fiercely protective of their own interests. The English Parliament had brought in restrictions on Irish exports, particularly cattle, which was the main source of Irish wealth. The Irish were also deprived of trading with the colonies. In 1699 the English Parliament, in a move to protect their own thriving woollen industry, prohibited the Irish from exporting their manufactured wool to any country whatever. This was a crushing blow for the Irish economy. It was also a slap in the face for the Irish ascendancy class. They had installed themselves as the master race in Ireland but to the English they were the underlings. To add salt to the settlers' wounded pride, Irish Parliament conducted their business subject to their discussions being monitored by the English and their decisions having to be ratified by the English Parliament. Mitchel, in his *History of Ireland*, summed up the situation: "In short, the Irish Parliament was soon to be taught that it was the mere agent of the English empire, and must aspire to no other freedom than the freedom to oppress and trample upon the ancient Irish nation." Lack of power in their own jurisdiction encouraged a sense of nationalism among the new gentry. But the Irish Parliament steered a careful course avoiding unnecessary confrontation with the English interest in Ireland or the ruling establishment in England. The more vigorous pursuit for greater autonomy and the presence of a purer form of patriotism was in short supply on the Irish political scene. Mostly it was to be found elsewhere.

William Molyneux, a graduate of Trinity College, a correspondent with Locke, the philosopher, and founder of the Dublin Philosophical Society, became the voice of settler protest. This protest was much more audible for most of the next century than Catholic unrest. Molyneux published his *Case of Ireland's Being Bound by Acts of Parliament in England, Stated* in 1698. It argued that Ireland was not subject to English parliament, that Ireland was a separate kingdom with equal rights to self-determination and that while it enjoyed the benefits of Magna Carta and English Common law it did so 'by the free Consent, Allowance and Acceptance of the People of Ireland'. The pamphlet outraged English sensitivities on the issue of sovereignty and was ordered to be publicly burnt by the hangman.

The Dublin Philosophical Society was founded in 1683, and its membership comprised mostly of graduates of Trinity College. Prominent figures included Narcissus Marsh, of Marsh Library fame, destined to become Archbishop of Dublin and then Primate of Ireland based in Armagh. William Petty (1623-87), compiler of the *Down Survey*, was its first President. The Society had three periods of activity from 1683-7, 1692-8 and 1707-8. It had links with the Royal Society, London, and was the forerunner of the Dublin Society. George Berkeley was a member in its last brief resurgence in 1707-8 and Thomas Prior may also have been involved at this time. He was certainly influenced by members of the Society, many of whom went on to join the Dublin Society he founded in 1731, a notable exception being Berkeley.

Swift and others would restate the case made by Molyneux in the years ahead and in the latter part of the 18th century Henry Grattan would carry it a step further. Prior was among these. His case, however, was based not on theory but on practical issues intended to improve Ireland's economy and raise the living standards of all in the country, not just the chosen few. His *List of Absentees* was to be a groundbreaking publication and one of the most important commentaries and economic assessments of 18th century Ireland. In it, he focuses his criticisms for the poor state of country not on the English, not on the Catholics, but on his own people – the landlord class – whom, he believed, were responsible for bankrupting the country and spending the fruits of their idleness abroad instead of at home where investment was so badly needed.

A glimmer of enlightenment had appeared in the midst of over-whelming darkness. If, as Lecky recognised, there was an immense preponderance of legislative power concentrated in the hands of a few, these few, as represented in the Irish parliament, or for the most part in the Irish Church, were unfortunately not the enlightened ones. The constitution of the Irish House of Commons was such that it did not represent the vast bulk of the Irish people, nor did it seek to do so. In law, the Catholics did not exist except for punishment purposes. Of the 300 members, 216 were elected by boroughs or manors, and of these, according to a conservative estimate, 176 were elected by individual patrons. Members concerned themselves with imaginary Catholic conspiracies and the securing of sinecures for relations and friends. The Church, supported by tithes, perpetuated an elaborate system of patronage and "was distinguished by lethargy, intellectual paralysis and jobbery".[7] The enlightened ones, mainly with Trinity backgrounds and well-versed in the scientific advances and philosophical thinking of the age, rarely locked horns with Parliament. There were practical reasons for not wanting to deliberately upset either the M.P.s or the adminstration. The selfishness and persecution complex that prevailed in the corridors of power did not leave much room for enlightenment and it had to find expression elsewhere. Through writings, debates and friendships with like-minded people, a new sense of patriotism was created, which found an appropriate forum in the Dublin Society.

Prior has been described as a "studious and intelligent young man" who participated in the cultural life of the College.[8] Writing some twenty years after his death, Pool and Cash state, "Mr. Prior being of a weak habit of body, declined entering any of the learned professions, though well qualified to have shone in them, but entirely turned his thoughts and studies to promote the real happiness of his country." Prior may not have been endowed with a robust physique but he went on to live a long and active life and there is little evidence to be found that he had any serious or lasting health problems.

After graduating in 1703 Prior retained close links with Trinity College and numerous documents give that as his address as late as 1716.[9] In 1712 Prior was in England. He went to Oxford University where he was incorporated an M.A. on 14 July of that year. He kept in close touch with his uncle, Richard, at Cambridge, over the years and it is believed that he spent some time with him on this visit before heading to London. His trip to the capital was, apparently, by arrangement to meet with Berkeley, who had taken leave of absence from Trinity College, where he lectured. It was probably here that he first met with Jonathan Swift.

Swift, like Prior and Berkeley, was educated at Kilkenny and Trinity College. In 1707 he was sent to London as emissary of the Irish clergy seeking remission of tax on Irish clerical incomes. His requests were rejected, however, by the Whig government and by Queen Anne. While in London, he met Hester van Homrigh, who would become the Vanessa of his writings. He had already become well known as a writer and satirist. His first work of note was *Tale of a Tub*, a prose satire on the religious extremes represented by Roman Catholicism and Calvinism. His *Battle of the Books* based on whether the works of the "Ancients" were to be preferred to those of the "Moderns" added to his growing fame. When in London he moved in top literary and political circles. Disgusted with their alliance with the Dissenters and policy on Church matters, Swift fell out with the Whigs and allied himself with the Tories. He introduced Berkeley to prominent figures at the Court of St. James on 12 April 1713, including Lord Berkeley of Stratton. The young Berkeley was introduced to his titled namesake in the typical Swiftian manner: "My Lord", he said "here is a fine young gentleman of your family. I can assure your Lordship it is a much greater honour to you to be related to him, than it is to him to be related to you." Lord Berkeley was impressed with the young man and they remained close acquaintances for many years.

That same year Berkeley published his *Three Dialogues between Hylas and Philonous* and this added to his reputation as a budding philosopher. Berkeley soon became a Court favourite. Swift was involved with the Scriblerus Club, a group of Tory satirists, whose members included Pope, Congreve, Gay and Arbuthnot. Berkeley met and conversed with these literary giants and through him Prior too, no doubt, came to know them and others of London's intellectual elite. Berkeley was a busy man and stayed on in London for some time. He asked Prior to manage his Irish affairs, which he had neglected. Helping out Berkeley family members was to be one of Prior's first assignments. These instructions directed Prior on his return to Dublin to send £40 to his brother, Cornet William Berkeley, quartered in Sligo, and to another sibling "Robin" (afterwards Dr. Robert Berkeley) several larger sums.[10]

By the end of 1713, Swift was installed as Dean of St. Patrick's Cathedral, Berkeley had left for Sicily as chaplain to the ambassador, Lord Peterborough, and Prior had settled back into Dublin's business life. On 25 November Berkeley wrote to Prior from Paris giving a full account of his journey and telling him of a visit to Father Malebranche, the disciple of Descartes, with whom he discoursed "on several points".[11] Berkeley had reached Turin in January and the following month he corresponded from Leghorn, requesting "a particular account of all transactions in Dublin and London".

Berkeley's letters reveal something of what preoccupied Prior's mind at the time. He was a young man of some means and contemplating his future. He did not fancy the idle life of leisure to which many young men of his class gravitated. He contemplated a grand tour through France and Italy, which Berkeley mapped out for him. For a time he entertained the idea of seeking a consular or diplomatic appointment and urged Berkeley to use his influence to this end. Berkeley mentioned the matter to the British Ambassador in Paris, who happened to be Matthew Prior, the poet and politician, but nothing came of it.[12] This was a rare, if not unique occasion, for Prior to seek a favour of a personal nature. All his representations in the future years would be in seeking to further lofty aims for improving the country's economy and, through his association with the Dublin Society, for the public good.

Although he was not as attentive to his own affairs as he might have been, Prior was a shrewd businessman. In a matter of a few years, he had established himself as town agent for many landowners. Clarke fills us in on some of his business dealings around this time. About 1716 he took a lease on hundreds of acres in County Wicklow which he sublet in smaller farms. His leases were models for the period. He insisted, for instance, upon the proper enclosure of lands by trenching and planting of quickthorns; laying down specifications for proper dwelling houses and the sowing of plantations; he even insisted in at least one lease that the tenant should have his corn ground "at Mr. Prior's mill at Arklow". He also owned part of the family estate at Rathdowney and on the death of his brother circa 1718 the remainder of the estate passed to him, but it would appear to have been heavily mortgaged. About this time his yearly income from his estates was more than £500.[13]

Berkeley again visited continental Europe in the 1716-20 period. He was appointed Dean of Dromore and Dean of Derry on his return. His appointment to Dromore committed him to a long lawsuit. He fell in for a share in the legacy of Hester van Homrigh estimated at £3,000, for reasons which remain inexplicable. Robert Marshall, a young lawyer, whom Clarke believed was at times apparently a business partner of Prior's, also benefited from the legacy. Berkeley now set his mind on establishing a new world mission and college in Bermuda and, having come to the belief that the government would support the plan, he and his new wife set sail for America in September 1728.

Mystery clouds a visit to Dublin earlier that year. He had written to Prior proposing to go to Dublin and that while he was there he would take the name of Mr. Brown. He desired to stay within a half mile of the town, where no one would know or observe him for half-a-year. Secrecy was most important; and he recalled a little white house on the hills near Rathmines that would suit him. The secret visit is likely to be connected to the fate of his brother, Thomas, who had been condemned to death for bigamy in 1726. The information appears in a letter dated 20 August 1726 from Knightly Chetwood to a John Ussher, F.T.C., of Dublin:

"Robin Leslie is at last arrived and has visited me. He resolves to go next April to Bermuda with George Berkeley, whose brother, a Bachelor of Arts in the College, I hear married two wives, one of them (the first) a cousin of Whitshed who condemned him at Kilkenny to die".

Berkeley's Bermuda project has fascinated scholars of this period over the years. Luce tells of Berkeley's dream to "build a St. Paul's College in the romantic, salubrious, unspoiled isles of Bermuda ... The sons of American settlers would be brought thither from the mainland, and when imbued with a sound Christian education they would be sent back to evangelise their homes".[14]

The success of the project was dependent on adequate financing. Van Homrigh's legacy was according to Berkeley a "providential event" and £5,000 had been subscribed privately. But he needed more, much more, to succeed. The shortfall would be met with a parliamentary grant. The House of Commons voted £20,000 to the project on 11 May 1726. The warrant was signed but still not sealed on the death of the King in June, 1727. Within a month, however a new warrant signed and sealed was secured from the new King, George II. The payment of the grant was delayed and eventually Berkeley sailed for America, expecting the money to come through at a later date. He set up house in Rhode Island with a view to establishing a college in Bermuda. It seems that he miscalculated the practical problems caused by the distance of 600 miles between Rhode Island and the islands of his dreams in the Atlantic. The Government grant never materialised and Berkeley's project came under criticism at home. Prior named him (the Dean of Derry) in his second edition of the *List of Absentees* as possessor of £900 a year spent out of Ireland. Berkeley's inclusion on the infamous "List" did not damage his friendship with Prior but apparently it caused the Bishop of Down to write him "a rude letter calling his scheme idle and simple, ordering him home, and asking were not the Irish Papists on his conscience".[15]

Berkeley knew his mission was doomed and he returned to London, arriving on 30 October 1731. But when his own project for the advancement of America failed, he did his best to further the interests of her existing seats of learning. He sent donations of collections of books to Yale and Harvard. The Rector of Yale, in 1766, described the donation to that college as "the finest collection of books that ever came together at one time into America".[16]

On his return Berkeley immediately published the celebrated *Alciphron or the Minute Philosopher*, the result of his studies in America. He followed this up with his *Theory of Vision, or Visual Language Vindicated and Explained* and in 1734 with *The Analyst*, in

14

which he criticised the position of the new mathematics which, in his view, were connected with a materialistic conception of the world. He had many admirers, including the King, George II, and Queen Caroline. They were decided that Berkeley must be a bishop but to make him a bishop in England "would revolt the whole clergy" warned Gibson, the Bishop of London, a friend of Berkeley. Despite jealousies in Ireland of Berkeley, it was decided to give him an Irish bishopric and in early 1734 he was appointed Bishop of Cloyne, in County Cork.

Prior, who was now immersed in his work for the Dublin Society which had been founded three years earlier, was still managing Berkeley's complicated financial affairs. His personal commitments were also increased by reason of the legacy from his Uncle Richard, who died at Ely in 1726. He was executor and trustee appointed under the will. Richard bequeathed to "his loving nephew Thomas Prior" some forty acres in the parish of Leverington in the Isles of Ely, and the lease-hold estate in the town of Cambridge called by the name of the "Green Dragon" also "the more-houses holden of the masters, fellows and scholars of St. John's College in the University of Cambridge". Prior sent Berkeley whatever information he could find on Cloyne and procured for him and his family lodgings at Gervais (Jervis) Street, on his arrival in Dublin, with accommodation for three man-servants and a private stable for six coach horses.[17] On 19 May, 1734, Berkeley was consecrated Bishop of Cloyne at St. Paul's Church, North King Street, Dublin. The ceremony was performed by three bishops, those of Cashel, Raphoe (his wife's uncle) and Killaloe.

References

(1) *Life of George Berkeley* by J. Hone and N. Rossi. 1938.
(2) ibid.
(3) ibid.
(4) ibid.
(5) ibid.
(6) *A History of Ireland in the Eighteenth Century* by W. E. H. Lecky. Chicago, U.S.A. 1972.
(7) ibid.
(8) *Thomas Prior* (1681-1751) by Desmond Clarke. Dublin. 1951.
(9) ibid.
(10) As (1).
(11) As (8)
(12) ibid.

(13) ibid.

(14) *Berkeley's Bermuda Project* by A. A. Luce (Proceedings of the Royal Academy, Vol. XL11, Section C, No. 6). Dublin. 1934.

(15) As (1).

(16) As (14). Berkeley's name is inextricably linked with the nurturing of university education in the U.S.A. Although his own ambitious Bermuda project failed, his early support for the Yale and Harvard institutions has made him a revered figure in that country. The University of California bears his name.

(17) As (1).

George Berkeley

CHAPTER 3

The List of Absentees

The Irish economy was in decline in the opening decades of the eighteenth century. The Anglo-Irish became increasingly incensed with restrictions imposed on Irish trade by the English Parliament. The banning of all exports of woollen products by an act of 1699 particularly infuriated them. England's political control fuelled the feeling of discontent, provoking the Anglo-Irish to demand greater charge over their own affairs. But their voice was often faint-hearted and their case was invariably dismissed by the English government. Bad harvests were a regular occurrence which deflated incomes for landowners. Good harvests deflated prices. For landowners it was a no-win situation. For the landless poor the situation was worse, much worse. Famine was never too far away.

Lord Molesworth, friend of William Molyneux, presented a good assessment of the economic stagnation and suggested remedies in his pamphlet *Some Considerations for Promoting Agriculture and Employing the Poor*, published in 1723. He was alive to the worst features of Irish agriculture – jobbing in land by middlemen who sub-let at a profit to the ruin of the farm and farmer alike. He suggested changes in the law for landlord and tenant. He could not understand how Irish farming methods had fallen so far behind England where tenants paid double the rent to their landlords and yet were able to make a handsome profit. He also had a social conscience, which was unusual for the gentry of the period. He wrote, "I know of no country where the real poor are worse taken care of". Among his recommendations were the setting up of "Schools of Husbandry" in every county run on a non-sectarian basis, teaching only good farming and good manners and that the children should daily serve God according to their own religion. Molesworth's pamphlet "exposed with a skilful and unsparing hand the gross defects of the Irish agricultural economy and at the same time proposed a series of remedies, which, if they had been carried out, ought to have made Ireland a happier and prosperous country".[1] Molesworth presented a solid case but it was clouded in the puritanical thinking of his class and time. He advocated tax reliefs for farmers and the poor 'who are over-burdened with children' but goes on to recommend such relief only to children who were the product of matrimony.

The shortage of small coin in the country caused particular problems for smaller business transactions and compounded the manifold hard-ships of the poor. England's answer was Wood's halfpence. The decision proved a disaster. William Woods, a Wolverhampton manufacturer, was granted the patent to mint £100,800 worth of debased copper coin for Ireland. There was uproar. The House of Commons and House of Lords in Ireland both passed hostile resolutions, and the lords justice, the privy council and the revenue commissioners resisted pressure to use the coinage. Swift with bitter irony fanned the flames of resistance to the foisting of the debased coinage on Ireland. His *Drapier Letters*, the first of which appeared in 1724, "added fuel to the smouldering fires and aroused a new spirit of independence in a spiritless people, and in the Irish parliament".[2] English Prime Minister, Sir Robert Walpole, realised the danger of allowing the issue of Ireland's political insubordination spiralling out of control. The patent was cancelled but Walpole was determined that such resistance from Ireland be nipped in the bud. He immediately initiated a policy that ensured that a proportion of key posts (including the lord chancellorship and the archbishopric of Armagh) were to be filled in future by politically reliable Englishmen. The appointment of Hugh Boulter (1671-1742), bishop of Bristol, to the arch-bishopric of Armagh in 1724 reflected the government's concern to tighten control on Irish affairs. He worked closely with a succession of lord lieutenants and was the *de facto* ruler of Ireland for almost two decades. He was "a bitter enemy of the Catholics"[3] and totally commit-ted to upholding the English interest at all times. He pressed for the appointment of English-born holders of office in Church and state and warned against what he saw as the nationalist pretensions of Irish Protestants.

Unlike Molesworth, who concentrated on economic and social issues, Swift's writings were a red-hot mixture of economics and politics. In his *Proposal for the Use of Irish Manufactures*, which was published anonymously, Swift set out his stall for Irish nationality. In it he urged people to reject "everything wearable that comes from England". His message was "burn everything English except their coal" – a slogan that was to used by de Valera and his republican Fianna Fail government in the Anglo-Irish economic war over two centuries later. The English inter-est was incensed and the printer was prosecuted. Nine times the jury returned a verdict of not guilty and such was the official urgency to make an example of the printer that nine times the Chief Justice with the temptingly misspellable name, Whitshed, sent it back demanding a guilty verdict. So unpopular were the proceedings, however, that it was decided to drop the charges and the printer was discharged.

Resentment against the selling of English goods grew in intensity in the years ahead and led to unrest. In one incident, several shops in Dublin were broken into by a mob of weavers from the Liberties seeking out English manufactures. Violence ensued and one of the weavers was fatally injured in a clash with the army which had been called out to deal with the emergency.[4]

The *Drapier Letters* made Swift a celebrated figure among the Anglo-Irish. De Vere White in his history of the Royal Dublin Society, however, had a different opinion of Swift's entitlement to hero status. "The impact of Swift's writing was out of all comparison with that of the less celebrated pamphleteers who wrote at the same time." Prior was foremost amongst these "less celebrated pamphleteers". De Vere White was "doubtful whether [Swift's] blasting irony achieved any practical result save the withdrawal of Wood's ha'pence which were badly needed and would have done no harm if their tainted origin had not been advertised".

McLoughlin accuses Swift of an ambiguity in Irish matters. "A champion against the oppressor, he neglects much more obvious and immediate examples of oppression. His is an Irish voice, but minority Irish. His target here is England's political mismanagement and neglect of Irish Protestant interests; it has nothing to say about the way England treats the Catholic majority. When the Drapier turns in his last letter to 'the poorer sort of our natives', his advice reads like the report of a colonial governor on the uncivilised natives. He speaks one kind of language when facing the English across the Irish Sea, but when he looks westward into Ireland the 'blest Patriot' sounds very different".[5]

In his *Drapier Letters,* Swift coined the admirable assertion that "government without the consent of the governed is the very definition of slavery". Swift was, of course, referring to the Protestant people of Ireland. One must wonder how a man of his genius could seem to overlook the situation of the Irish Catholics. By his own definition they were the slaves of slaves. But to him, and to most of the New English, the comparison between Protestants and Catholics could not be made because Catholics, by law, did not exist. They were, for political purposes, invisible. Swift's blinkered vision of political rights was typical of Anglo-Irish thinking of the day. McDowell comments on this invisibility: "It is remarkable how the members of this proud community were able to ignore the existence of their helots".[6]

A

L I S T

OF THE

ABSENTEES

OF

I R E L A N D,

AND THE

YEARLY VALUE

OF THEIR

ESTATES and INCOMES

Spent Abroad.

WITH

OBSERVATIONS

On the PRESENT

Trade and Condition

OF THAT

KINGDOM.

The Second EDITION. With an APPENDIX.

Vincit Amor Patriæ. VIRGIL.

D U B L I N:
Printed for R. GUNNE in *Capel-ſtreet.* M DCC XXIX.

TITLE PAGE OF THE SECOND EDITION OF PRIOR'S LIST OF ABSENTEES

The Anglo-Irish contemporary view of the native Irish was akin to that of a sub-human species. They were a lazy and dirty lot, the dregs of society, a burden and a danger to the ruling class. Molesworth, a moderate and a man with a social conscience, wrote of the poor Irish as "a race of people like gypsies, which no priest takes care of, yet are seminaries of all rebellions, dangerous in plague times, revengeful at all times". He also favoured the shipping of vagrants abroad and apprenticing their children to tradesmen at home.

Arthur Dobbs (1689-1765), the author of *Trade and Improvement of Ireland* published in 1729, had also something to say about the Irish poor. He suggested the idea of enforced apprenticeship and recommended that children of the poor should wear some sort of dog-collar. Humanity in early eighteenth century Ireland was an appreciably different concept than it is today. Dobbs was, like Molesworth, a moderate. He was a friend of Prior and was one of the founding members of the Dublin Society in 1731. He later explored the North-West Passage and became Governor of North Carolina. De Vere White was impressed with Dobbs' knowledge of the economy.[7] He believed, too, that his range of interests was wider than Prior's but pointedly commented that "he does not seem so selfless as Prior". De Vere White also considered that Prior's closest friend, Berkeley, "who is almost venerated today was so much a child of his age" regarding aspects of his social thinking particularly in relation to the children of the idle poor or the lawbreaker. "Berkeley", he states, "could notice with gratification that in Holland an infant of four was able to earn its own living in a workhouse and he wondered whether the spectacle of criminals 'chained in pairs and kept at hard labour' would not be 'very edifying to the multitude." Indeed, Berkeley in *The Querist*, first published in 1735, asked,"whether our old, native Irish are not the most indolent and supine people in Christendom?"

Prior, however, did not share with others around him the discouraging view of the native Irish. He described them as living "poor and cheap". In his best known work, *A List of Absentees*, he bitterly complained of a country that could produce and export huge quantities of beef, butter, tallows, hides and wool "and yet our Common People are very poorly clothed, go bare-footed half the year and very rarely taste of fleshment with which we so much abound". This is the language of a man with an acute social conscience, a rare if not unique quality for his class and time.

Prior was ever the practical down-to-earth man, instinctively zoning in on what he saw as the kernel of the problem. From what we know of him, from what he wrote and from what others wrote about him, he comes across as a reserved yet kindly and highly intelligent man. An innovator and a most able administrator, Prior was a good communicator and a man with his finger on the pulse of the present yet always with an eye on the future. Above all he was a modest, hard-working and self-effacing individual, a man with the moral courage to confront people of influence and power and point out the errors of their ways; a man who sought no personal gain nor public recognition for the work he was doing. He was an Irishman and felt an affinity for Ireland and it was his lifelong mission to make it a better country for all the people who lived in it.

De Vere White gave this assessment of Prior: "The 'son of an Englishman' was how he described himself, showing that he regarded himself as differing in this respect from his father – as being, in fact, Irish. His cast of mind was puritan, but he seems to have been free from self-righteous or bigoted opinions. … He was very busy and public-spirited, not very efficient in private business, but zealous in public affairs. Too busy, it would seem, to have time to marry; too useful, occupied and constructive to waste time in quarrels. He left behind him no trace of scandal or folly, and such references to him as exist speak only in his praise. His views were radical and he expressed them bravely. His pamphlets ensured him the disfavour of Government because not only did he criticise Irish affairs, but he also questioned conventional beliefs."[8]

Swift published his most popular and enduring work, *Gulliver's Travels*, in 1726. He followed this up the following year with yet another attack on government policies in his *Short View of the State of Ireland*. In 1729, after a succession of bad harvests causing famine amongst the Irish poor, he published his grotesque satire on overpopulation and food shortage, *A Modest Proposal*. His proposal was, rather, an "immodest" one. The plight of the Catholics was pitiful and while Swift could not see them as existing in political terms, he could not but be moved by the appalling conditions and suffering of the poor, subsisting on the fringe of society and dying in dire distress in hovels and on the roadside. His proposal was for "preventing children of poor people in Ireland from being a burden to their parents or country and for making them beneficial to the public". He suggests that infants and young children should be treated like common livestock. They are to be bred, fed, and then cooked in whatever way to feed the upper class of England. The children could also be used to make fashion accessories such as gloves, purses and belts. His rationale is that the number of Papists would be lessened, the poor would have goods to pay their bills and the food (children) would become a symbol of fine dining.

Swift's biting satire once again stirred controversy on the issue of nationalism and the economy but it was left to others to find the underlying reasons for the recurring famine and to suggest remedies. Prior was foremost of these. In the same year as Swift published his "modest" proposal, Prior published two important pamphlets on the economy. Both related to pet concerns of his. One was the shortage of coin and the other related to the drain on the economy of Irish revenue spent abroad. *Observations on Coin in General with some Proposals for regulating the Value of Coin in Ireland* deals not only with small coin but with the chaotic condition of all species of money in the country: "This was a matter in which Swift was not so keenly interested".[9] Apart from copper, there was also a shortage of silver and gold due to the depressed state of the economy, the lack of parity between English and Irish money which emanated from the same mint and Irish money spent abroad by absentees. Small silver coinage was very scarce while the Portuguese gold coin, the moidore, was in more common usage than the guinea. Swift had exaggerated the effects of Wood's halfpence and his outraged writings forced its withdrawal. But its cancellation still left Ireland with the problem of a shortage of small coin. Prior, in his pamphlet, revisits the issue in a less eloquent but more factual account of the coin shortage issue. "'Tis certain that at present we are far from having a sufficient quantity of Halfpence, which we are sensible of in all our Domestick Dealings, wherein we labour under great difficulties for small change in Copper Money. This Scarcity is a general complaint over all the Kingdom, and throws poor people into distress, disabling them in a great measure from carrying on their small dealings with one another, and their grievance is heightened by an absolute want of Farthings, of which we have hardly any in the Kingdom."

Prior had a good grasp of economics and educated himself well on the relative values of coinage and its importance to conducting business transactions. He writes on the theory of money and its relationship to international trade, sets down tables of assay, discusses comparative coin values and refers to Newton's reports on minting. He strongly supports the setting up of an Irish mint and advocates at least a limited parity on coin values between England and Ireland to offset the apparent trafficking of gold and silver coins between the two countries.

Prior's other pamphlet of 1729 on absentees was, however, the one to have the more profound impact. While Swift and other writers of the period had plenty to say about the disreputable poor, Prior made his target the disreputable rich. His *List of Absentees* – or to give it its full title *A List of Absentees of Ireland and the Yearly Value of their Estates and Incomes Spent Abroad with Observations On the Present Trade and Condition of That Kingdom* – exposed the large number of landowners who lived abroad spending money wrung from hard-pressed Irish tenants at home. It also exposed the evil system whereby English henchmen obtained government sinecures, and drew large salaries therefrom but refused to live in Ireland. It was a landmark publication and one which Prior knew would not make him popular with the government or among his own class. He saw a country that was being exploited by a selfish breed of people, some of whom were acquaintances and friends. The Irish economy was in tatters, being milked dry by those absentees who took all they could out of the country but chose to put nothing back in. This was a broadside, a publication that he knew would enrage the English and Anglo-Irish interest alike. It was the work of a man of commitment and courage. Prior did not seek any sinecures from officialdom or curry personal favours from the government or the Court. He was above reproach in this respect. His cold, clinical statistics, independent and radical views and clear logical conclusions struck a raw nerve with the establishment and their touts. It was certainly widely read. It was one of the most important publications in eighteenth century Ireland and was the most reprinted; a best-seller of the day.

Prior estimated that more than £600,000 was being siphoned from the country by absentees, who put nothing back into the economy. He suggested a tax of twenty per cent on the estates of absentees. "'Tis to be hoped that our Legislature will take care that those Gentlemen, who spend their fortunes abroad, are thereby the greatest, and almost only cause of its poverty and distress, shall not be the Persons favoured, and exempted from paying the taxes thereof. A tax of four shillings in the pound on the estates of Absentees, would in all likelihood, remove the evil complained of, by stopping in a grate (sic) measure those wasteful drains of our money."

He divided his list into three classes: "First Class comprehends those, who live constantly abroad, and are seldom, or never seen in Ireland. Second Class comprehends those, who live generally abroad, and visit Ireland now and then, for a Month or two. Third Class takes in those, who live generally in Ireland, but were occasionally absent, at the Time the said List was taken, either for Health, Pleasure, or Business; but their Number is commonly the same, and supply their Places."

Prior summarises the "Yearly Value Spent Abroad" as follows:

By those of the First Class	£204200 00 0
By those of the Second Class	91800 00 0
By those of the Third Class	54000 00 0
By those, whose income is under 400 l. per ann.	40000 00 0
By those, who have Employments in Ireland	31510 00 0
For the Education of Youth, Law-Suits, Attendance, and by Dealers	33000 00 0
By the Pensioners on the Civil List	23070 13 1
By those on the Military Est.	67658 10 0
By French Pensioners	2560 00 0
By Remittances to Gibraltar	30000 00 0
By Adventurers to America	30000 00 0
On Account of several Articles mentioned in the last Par.	20000 00 0
	£627799 03 1

Prior, in his *Observations on the Present Trade and Condition of the Country* appended to his "List", explains the relationship of money with commerce, the importance of exports and imports and of having a favourable balance of trade, the effect of rising interest rates on the availability of money and the impact of lost revenue due to absentees: "We are now at a loss to point out the principle source of all our Misfortunes, and the chief Cause of all this Distress; it appears plainly, from the List of Absentees, and the Estimate of the Quantity of Species, they may be reasonable supposed to draw yearly out of the Kingdom, that no other Country labours under so wasteful a Drain of its Treasure, as Ireland does at present, by an annual Remittance of above £600,000. to our Gentlemen abroad, without the least Consideration or Value return'd for the same: This is so great a Burthen upon us, that I believe, there is not in History, an Influence of any one Country, paying so large a yearly Tribute to another."

Prior goes on to warn that if the absentees continued to drain the country of its money then not only would it be bankrupt but so too would they themselves: "'Tis true, this Evil is of such a Nature, as in a little Time, it must cure itself; for if the Demands of our Absentees greatly exceed all our Gain by Trade, and amount to as much yearly, as the whole current Coin of the Kingdom; there will be soon nothing left for them to draw away, and they must be forc'd to return to their Native Country; which must necessarily be the Case, unless, (which cannot reasonably be supposed) they shall think it a less Grievance to starve abroad. ... When things come to this Extremity, Great must be the Calamity of all, even of those who are innocent, and have not the least Share in bringing this Evil upon us; for then, no Rents can be paid in Money, but all in Kind; no sort of Trade can be carried on, but by bartering one Commodity for another: The Price of Lands must universally fall, the Army must be broke, or live on free Quarters, and the Establishment, and all Professions must sink for Want of Money to support them."

This is impassioned writing, over the top by present day standards, but in order to claim the public's attention he deliberately laced his sound logic with particular illustrations of absenteeism. In one such personal reference, Prior quotes the case of a "well-known absentee who has by his rents and otherwise, drawn out of this Kingdom nearly £400,000L the last twenty years, and yet that same Lord has not contributed to the Support of Public Charges, as much as the meanest person, who pays for a quart of ale." He quotes another instance of blatant contempt for the Irish situation. It refers to the case of an Englishman "who having obtained an employment in Ireland, landed in Dublin on Saturday evening, went next day to a Parish Church and received the sacrament. On Monday morning he took the oaths in the Courts, and in the afternoon set sail for England again and we never saw more of him".

The author complains bitterly: "We pinch ourselves in every article of life, and export more than we can spare, with no other effect or advantage, than to enable our Gentlemen and Ladies to live more luxuriously abroad ... They are not content to treat us thus, but add insult to ill usage; they reproach us with our poverty, and at the same time they take away our money; and can tell us we have no Diversions or Entertainements in Ireland for them, when they themselves disable us from having better by withdrawing from us."

In the final paragraph of his "Observations", Prior defines the love of one's country and asks readers to be cautious at election time before voting for absentees: "The Love of one's Country is seldom found in any remarkable Degree, but in those, who live long in it, agreeable to the Intention of Nature, which disposes all Men and other Creatures to a Fondness for those Places in which they live; if this be the Case, I fear we can expect but little Good from those, who, by forsaking their Country, must have lost almost all natural Affection towards it; and this may teach us, who still retain a Sense of Duty we owe our Country, to be very cautious, on all future Elections of Parliament Men, or on any other Occasions, how we pay any Regard to those, who do not live constantly among us. It must be of Service, to take publick Notice of those Actions, which tend both, to the Good and Hurt of one's Country; in order to excite us to the Practice of the First, and prevent our being guilty of the Second."

In his pamphlet Prior expanded on his ideas for the improvement of trade, agriculture and industry. Apart from the excessive spending abroad, he was critical of "our immoderate consumption of foreign commodities". The return to pasturage and the drop in acreage under tillage aggravated the famine of 1729. Prior called for an extension of tillage and, despite restrictive legislation, saw no reason why the woollen industry should not be expanded to clothe the Irish people and he even suggested the use of woollen shrouds to clothe the dead. Over-production of wool should be rectified by feeding less sheep and planting the former pasture lands with flax. This would increase the production of linen, which would substitute for imported silks. He suggests madder and hops could be grown and industries started for the manufacture of paper, cambric, glass and earthware and that greater use should be made of Irish shipping.

Prior's belief that absenteeism was the major cause of Ireland's economic woes was never seriously challenged until long after his death in 1751. The problem of absentee landlords persisted into the nineteenth and, to some extent, twentieth centuries. In 1833, over a century after the first publication of the "List", Barrington wrote scathingly on the subject and in very much a similar vein to what Prior had written. "Absentees, who have ever been and ever will remain an obstacle to the substantial prosperity of Ireland. ... They knew their Irish demenses only by name and by income, they felt no interest but for their rents, and no patriotism but for the territory. ... (They are) a strenuous and weighty opposition to every measure of innovation. ... Alarmed at any legislative measure originating in Ireland, they showed themselves equally ignorant and regardless of her constitution, and ever proved themselves the steady adherents of the Minister of the time being; their proxies in the Lords, and their influences in the Commons, were transferred to him on a card or in a letter, and on every division in both houses, they almost invariably formed a phalanx against the true and genuine interest of the country." Barrington noted further: "The absentees of the present day annually draw from Ireland above three million sterling, to be expended in Great Britain. Some of the law-offices of the greatest emolument, connected with the Irish courts of justice, are now held by constant landlords."

Some more modern day writers believe that Prior overstated the extent of the problem of absentees. His assertion that "those Gentlemen, who spend their fortunes abroad, are thereby the greatest, and almost only cause of its poverty and distress" has been disputed. McCracken believes that the drain on the economy caused by the remittances to absentees was exaggerated. He estimates that in the 1720s probably about one quarter to one sixth of the total rent roll went to absentees and this probably had fallen to one eighth by the 1770s. He reckons that the extent to which absentees neglected their estates was also exaggerated. "Some of the larger estates owned by absentees were expertly managed by professional agents who were kept under close surveillance by the owners." He does admit, however, that "absenteeism was nonetheless an additional barrier between landlord and tenant in a country where there were already barriers in plenty."[10]

Lecky pulls no punches about the evils of absenteeism and particularly the breed of social animal it created – the middleman. "Absenteeism drew away a great part of the richer landlords, while the middlemen rapidly multiplied. A hybrid and ambiguous class, without any of the solid qualities of the English yeomen, they combined the education and manners of farmers with the pretensions of gentlemen, and they endeavoured to support these pretensions by idleness, extravagance, and ostentatious arrogance. Men who in England would have been modest and laborious farmers, in Ireland sub-let their land at rack-rents, kept miserable packs of half-starved hounds, wandered about from fair to fair and from race to race in laced coats, gambling, fighting, drinking, swearing, ravishing and sporting, parading everywhere their contempt for honest labour, giving a tone of recklessness to every society in which they moved. An industrial middle class, which is the most essential of all elements of English life, was almost totally wanting; and the class of middlemen and squireens, who most nearly corresponded to it, were utterly destitute of industrial virtues, and concentrated in themselves most of the distinctive vices of the Irish character. They were the chief agents in agrarian tyranny, and their pernicious influence on manners, in a country where the prohibition of manufactures had expatriated the most industrious classes and artificially checked the formation of industrial habits, can hardly be overrated … These are signs of a society profoundly diseased, and it is not difficult to trace the causes of the malady."[11]

Prior's "List" and "Observations" were not well received by Primate Boulter. Described by Lecky as "a narrow, intolerant and dull man", Boulter's concern was always the English interest. Prior's pamphlet prompted him to write to the Duke of Newcastle, then Prime Minister: "There is a very bad spirit, I fear, artfully spread among all degrees of men amongst us, and the utmost grumbling against England as getting all our money from us, either by trade or otherwise, and this spirit has been heightened by a book lately published here about absentees. … I believe among less intelligent persons they are for taxing the absentees four shillings in the pound; but I am satisfied that men of sense in either House are too wise to make any attempt of that nature, which they know could only exasperate England without even having such a Bill returned to us."

Prior's views and ideas fuelled interest and debate on ways to improve the dire economic condition of the country. He believed that the answer to many of the economic problems lay largely in Irish hands and appealed to other like-minded men to join him in a forum that would convert ideas into action. Thus was founded the Dublin Society in 1731.

References

(1) A quote from Lecky in *A History of the Royal Dublin Society* by Henry F. Berry. London. 1915.

(2) *Thomas Prior (1681-1751)* by Desmond Clarke. Dublin. 1951.

(3) *A History of Ireland in the Eighteenth Century* (Religion and Society) by W. E. H. Lecky. Chicago, U.S.A. 1972.

(4) *Consumer Nationalism in 18th Century Dublin* by Sarah Foster (History Today, June 1997)

(5) *Contesting Ireland – Irish Voices against England in the Eighteenth Century* by Thomas McLoughlin. Dublin. 1999.

(6) *Irish Public Opinion, 1750-1800* by R. B. McDowell. 1943.

(7) *The Story of the Royal Dublin Society* by Terence de Vere White. Tralee. 1955.

(8) ibid.

(9) As (2).

(10) Essay by J. L. McCracken on "The social structure and social life 1714-60" from *A New History of Ireland* vol. 1V edited by T. W. Moody and W. E. Vaughan.

(11) As (3).

Royal Dublin Society.

Facsimile of the first page of the first minute book

25ᵗʰ June 1731

CHAPTER 4

The Founding of the Dublin Society

O n 25 June 1731 fourteen men met in the rooms of the Philosophical Society in Trinity College and agreed to form a society for improving husbandry, manufactures and other useful arts. The following is a transcript of the minutes of that first meeting:

Dublin, 25th June, 1731

Present

Judge Ward, Sir Th. Molyneux, Th. Upton, Esq, Dr. Stephens, John Pratt, Esq, Rich. Warburton, Esq, Rev. Dr. Whitecomb, Arthur Dobs, Esq, Dr. Magnaten, Dr. (John) Madden, Dr. Lehunte, Mr. Walton, Mr. Prior and W. Maple.

Several gentlemen agreed to meet in the Philosophical Rooms in Trin. Col., Dub., in order to promote Improvements of all kinds, and Dr. Stephens being desired, took the Chair.

It was proposed and unanimously agreed unto, to form a Society, by the name of the Dublin Society, for improving Husbandry, Manufactures, and other useful arts.

It was proposed and resolved, that all the present, and all such who should become members of the Society, shall subscribe their names to a Paper, containing their agreement to form a Society for the purposes aforesaid.

Ordered that a Committee of all the members present do meet next Thursd., in the Philosophical Rooms in Trin. Col., Dub., to consider of a Plan or Rules for the Government of the Society, any three thereof to be a Quorum, and that notice be sent to the members in Town, the day before the time for the meeting. The Society adjourned to this day fort-night.

Henry F. Berry in his history of the Royal Dublin Society wrote admiringly of these fourteen founding members: "The names of those who thus stood round the cradle of the infant Society must ever be held in honour in this country, and, though all were men of note, the names of at least eight stand out prominently as having, from the start and for years after, laboured assiduously and unselfishly in promoting the ends it had in view. Primarily, they set themselves to educate those concerned in the first principles of successful farming, and in endeavouring to promote industries which might afford employment. … the warmest admiration must be felt for them as men who seemed so much in advance of their age, and who aimed at making Ireland not only self-supplying, but also a great exporting country."

The eight men Berry picks out for special mention are:

Michael Ward, of Castle Ward, Co. Down, M.P. for the county of Down 1715; Justice of the King's Bench 1727-'59.

Sir Thomas Molyneux, brother of William Molyneux, born in Dublin in 1661. Fellow of the Royal Society he became President of the Irish College of Physicians in 1702. Friend of Robert Boyle and Sir William Petty and in London became acquainted with Sir Isaac Newton, John Evelyn, Dryden and Locke.

Rev. Dr. John Whitecombe, born in Cork. Tutor to Lord George Sackville, son of the Duke of Dorset, to whom he was chaplain. Appointed Bishop of Clonfert in 1735, then Bishop of Down and Connor and in 1752 Archbishop of Cashel, where he is buried in the old cathedral.

Arthur Dobbs, was Engineer in chief and Surveyor-general in Ireland and M.P. for Carrickfergus in the Parliament of 1727-'60. He advocated an improved system of land tenure and published his essay on the *Trade and Improvement of Ireland* in 1729. He followed it up with a pamphlet *Thoughts on Government in general in 1731*. He promoted the search for a North-West passage to China and India and Cape Dobbs in Hudson Bay is named in his honour. In 1754 he was appointed Governor of North Carolina.

William Stephens, was physician to the Royal Hospital in Dublin and was also physician to Mercer's and Steevens' Hospitals. In 1733 he became lecturer in Chemistry in Trinity College and became President of the College of Physicians that year and again in 1742.

Francis Le Hunte, M.D., succeeded his brother Richard in the family estates in Co. Wexford. Having retired from his medical practice he moved to Dublin where he became involved in numerous charities and was known and loved as a benevolent and affable man.

William Maple, a distinguished chemist at the University of Dublin and keeper of Parliament House. In 1727 the Irish Parliament presented him with £200 for discovering a new method of tanning leather. Rhames printed his *A Method of Tanning without Bark* in 1729. One of Prior's longtime associates and closest friends, Maple was curator and registrar to the Dublin Society until his death at the remarkable age of 104 in 1762.

The eighth member (seventh on Berry's list) selected for special mention was Thomas Prior. None are singled out in Berry's account published in 1915 as outstanding above another but de Vere White was more forthcoming in his history published four decades later. On his authority Prior was the prime mover in founding the society. He believed that without Prior there would have been no Royal Dublin Society.

Clarke asks us to "pause for a moment to see 'what manner of men' were they who, voluntarily and with no purpose but to serve their country, gathered together to found and establish a Society, which the same voluntary effort has sustained for over two hundred years. These men were of the same Anglo-Irish stock as Prior; they were imbued with the same ideas and ideals as he was, and they have almost without exception, in some sphere or other, left their imprint."[1]

If Prior was the main driving force behind the foundation of the Dublin Society, Clarke acknowledges that William Maple, "perhaps after Prior" was the most indefatigable supporter and bemoans his absence from the *Dictionary of National Biography*. As keeper of Parliament House he enabled the Society members to hold their early meetings in a room there and it was in a cellar in the same building that he opened the first museum of agricultural instruments in these islands.

Of the other founder members, Richard Warburton, Thomas Upton, Mr. Walton and John Pratt were all extensive landowners. Dr. Magnaten (later spelled MacNaghten) was a well-known Dublin physician who was known for his generosity to the poor. John Madden, Clarke informs us, was also a physician and a brother-in-law of William and Thomas Molyneux. But the de Vere White history of the R.D.S. and the later one edited by James Meenan and Clarke and published in 1981, at which time Clarke was dead, tell us that Madden was a clergyman of the Established Church and does not mention the relationship with Molyneux. His name has often been confused with Molyneux's nephew, the Rev. Samuel Madden whom, de Vere White notes, was never a member but through his premium schemes was very supportive of the Society in the early years.

The Rev. John Madden, who was Vicar of St. Anne's in Dawson Street, Dublin, attended the first meeting, but played no further part in the story of the RDS. He is best remembered rather as the victim of a practical joke played by the Earl of Rosse as related by de Vere White. "Dr. Madden was greatly perturbed to hear that Lord Rosse, who had led a very unsaintly life, was on his deathbed. Being a zealous clergyman, he wrote a long letter to the dying Lord, recalling his sins, urging repentance, and offering to call. Lord Rosse redirected the letter to Lord Kildare, a pious family man, living in the same parish. Lord Kildare, outraged, went to the Bishop, showed him Dr. Madden's letter and demanded satisfaction. By the time the comedy had played itself out, Lord Rosse was dead. As Dr. Madden afterwards became Dean Of Kilmore, he suffered no lasting hurt for is apparent indiscretion; and we must hope that Lord Rosse was able to work out his salvation without Dr. Madden's assistance."[2]

The second meeting of the Dublin Society was held a week later on 1st July, 1731. Prior chaired the meeting and, without waiting for officers to be elected or a constitution to be approved, straightaway got down to business. He and Dr. Stephens were requested to draw up the rules of the Society which were submitted and rubber-stamped at a later meeting. The admission fee was fixed at £1.10s and the annual subscription was set at the same figure. At this meeting it was decided to add "Sciences" after "Arts" in the title of the Society. Dr. Stephens presented 2,000 copies of the Society's aims and objectives for distribution. He also gave a lecture on dyeing. Rhames was elected printer for the Society and was instructed to reprint Jethro Tull's "Horse Hoeing Husbandry", the most informed work on ploughing at the time. Berry surmised that the Irish edition "appears to be a clear case of piracy, as the work had only just appeared in England". The members of the Society did not appear to share Berry's concern regarding copyright. Tull (1674-1741) had revolutionised agriculture in England and there was great enthusiasm within the infant organisation to spread the good news in Ireland.

On 30th September, 1731, Prior submitted a paper on *A New Method of draining Marshy and Boggy lands*. His essay was illustrated with diagrams and is attached to the original minute book. This was the first paper read and discussed at a meeting of the Society. At the next meeting a paper on *Hampshire Methods in the Culture of Hops* was presented by Captain Cobbe and read by Prior. Prior was a strong advocate of growing crops like hops and madder at home and both crops are mentioned in his *List of Absentees*. He later published a treatise on hop growing, which for almost half a century was considered the authoritative work on the subject.[3] Despite his sustained efforts hop growing never won widespread appeal in this country. On 18 November, 1731, Prior presented the first series of questions relating to madder and the desirability of dyeing cloth at home instead of sending it to Holland and France for this purpose. Queries were forwarded to Holland to elicit information on the subject. Dutch methods seem to have been highly appreciated, and amongst the earliest volumes acquired by the Society as a nucleus for its library were works by Dutch writers on agriculture and husbandry. Prior also submitted a paper from a Mr. Stothard on the *Cultivation of Rye*. Members also interested themselves in the cultivation of flax. Despite extensive experimenting, the growing of flax never took hold in the south of the country although it became a major industry in the north.

Between the founding of the Society in June and its first A.G.M. in December twenty-six members joined. The membership was predominated by doctors at first but five Bishops added their names to the growing list. Two notable names missing from the list are Prior's *alter ego*, George Berkeley,[4] who returned to London from his Bermuda project in America in October, 1731, and Dean Swift, "who had become tired and peevish".[5] Both men kept themselves well briefed on the proceedings of the Society, however, and Berkeley was particularly supportive and cooperated in many of the Society's projects. His predecessor in the Bishopric of Cloyne, Edward Synge, and close friend, Sir John Percival, became early members. So too did Frederick Lucas, Lord Mountcashel, Robert Clayton, Bishop of Clogher, and Dr. Patrick Delany, husband of the famous letter-writer.

At the meeting of 4 December, 1731, The Lord Lieutenant,The Duke of Dorset (Lionel Cranfield Sackville) was elected President; the Primate, Hugh Boulter, became Vice-President; Secretary for Home Affairs was Dr. Stephens; Anthony Shepherd (Junior), Treasurer; William Maple, Curator and Registrar; and with the grandiose title of Secretary for Foreign Affairs, Thomas Prior. Although by this early stage the Society had made little impact either at home or abroad, the need to get the latest information and knowledge from more progressive countries like Holland and England and apply this to the Irish situation, backward in agricultural and industrial know-how, was felt vital. Prior searched widely for knowledge and advice but did not confine himself to foreign matters. Effectively, as secretary, he ran the Society for the next twenty years and "little was done or achieved without his advice, help and active cooperation".[6]

The Lord Lieutenant or Primate Boulter took no part in the Society's activities. Lord Lieutenants came and went but Primate Boulter remained a towering figure on the Irish scene for a long period. As Archbishop of Armagh he remained the most powerful man in Ireland from 1724 to 1742. Lecky describes him well: "He watched with an eager, cat-like vigilance every sign of decaying health, that made it probable that some great man would soon drop from his post, and sometimes even before the catastrophe, sprang forward to secure the place for an Englishman." De Vere White illustrates, in an amusing aside, the Primate's all-abiding concerns as an Englishman: "The Archbishop of Cashel was having his leg massaged with brandy by his wife: the spirits took fire and the result was very unpleasant for his Grace. Boulter conveying the sad news to London cannot forbear to add: 'if he dies … fill the place with some Englishman that is already on the Bench here'." Boulter was suspicious of all who promoted the Irish interest. The foremost of these, Prior, had come to his notice only a few years previously. As mentioned in the previous chapter, his *List of Absentees* had concerned the Primate sufficiently to warn the Prime Minister of the subterfuge contained in the publication against the English interest. The Society, and Prior, in particular, apparently made a point never again to offend the Primate's sensibilities, if at all possible, and Boulter, during his term in Armagh, did not contribute and, more importantly, did not interfere in the workings of the Society.

At a meeting on 18 December, 1731, the "Rules for the Regulation of the Dublin Society" were adopted. There were twenty in all and two more were added the following month. Rule number one provided that the "election of member, after 100 shall have subscribed, shall be by Ballot". Some rules clearly defined the role of the Committee and the officers while others were quite specific on ways to promote the aims of the Society.

There was a rule, for instance, which allowed the Committee of Arts to "admit artists, tradesmen, and husbandmen, to assist and inform the members, in such Arts and improvements as shall be thought useful, and fit to be encouraged and propagated in the kingdom".

Another rule stated "that it be the business of the Committee of Arts, particularly to enquire into the state of Husbandry and the several mechanic Arts in this kingdom" while yet another provided for the procurement of models of the most advanced instruments and engines in use in other countries.

The influence of Thomas Prior is apparent in the composition of the rules. It is especially evident in those that encourage active member participation in furthering the aims of the Society. Rule 19 stated "that every member of this Society, at his admission, be desired to choose some particular subject, either in Natural History, or in Husbandry, Agriculture, or Gardening, or some species of Manufacture, or other branch of improvement, and make it his business, by reading what had been printed on that subject, by conversing with them who made it their profession, or by making his own experiments, to make himself master thereof, and to report in writing, the best account they can get by experiment or enquiry relating thereunto."

Rule 20 regulated on how best to communicate the fruits of this research to other members and "when well considered and approved of, be printed for the use of the public, in order that the skill, manner of work, and the instructions made use of in other countries, or in some parts of this kingdom only, may be transferred and set up in other places, where they are not known, or improved in such manner as they are capable of".

Prior kept himself busy with the business of the Society and in encouraging other members to actively participate. He submitted an abstract of Slater and Hall's pamphlet, *Directions in saving and raising Flax and Flaxseed* at a meeting on 24 February, 1732. The abstract was published under the title *Advantages which may arise to the people of of Ireland by raising of Flax and Flaxseed, Considered, together with instructions for sowing and saving the Seed, and preparing the Flax for the Market. Drawn up and published by the Direction of the Dublin Society*. This was one of the many pamphlets in which, according to Clarke, "his hand can be traced" which deals with industries he believed could be successfully fostered in Ireland.[7]

By the second year the library of books acquired on various topics and from various sources was growing steadily. So too were the numbers and variety of agricultural implements and models which were housed in the vaults of the Irish Parliament House. A catalogue was drawn up of all the books of husbandry and mechanic arts in English, French, Greek and Latin. The Arts Committee were also asked to ascertain what books in foreign languages gave the best account of same, as practised in France, Flanders, Holland, Germany, Poland and Italy. As Berry notes: "A very practical suggestion was also made and carried out, namely that letters be sent to correspondents in the country to engage them to form local societies in the principal towns and cities, for the promotion of husbandry and agriculture, which might establish communications with the Dublin Society."[8] A set of Maps of Ireland by Grierson was ordered to be purchased.

Topics discussed at the fortnightly meetings were wide-ranging. The cultivation of apples for cider making was a popular subject. Members felt the climate and soil in the south of the country were particularly favourable for apple growing. Experiments were conducted on saffron growing and on methods of cleansing corn and clover grass seed. Copies of Slater's *Culture of Flax*, received from the Linen Board, were distributed.

At a meeting in February a letter was read from a William Colles, of Kilkenny, which informed the Society that he had secured an interest in a quarry of black marble together with some mills on the river. As a result of experiments "he had now ten saws moved by water power, working day and night. ... An engine ground the marble with sand, to fit it for polishing ... and he employed thirty hands in turning out chimney pieces, tables, mortars, tombstones, &c . He had also brought to perfection the boring of marble pipes, which served to convey water underground and from the tops of houses."[9] Members were impressed. A paper was presented on Colonel Prittie's silver mines in County Tipperary, which had been leased to an English company.

Members certainly took Rule 19 to heart. Many became experts in the most extraordinary subjects, particularly some of the clergymen members. The Bishop of Down (Dr. Francis Hutchinson) was invited to present a paper on Bogs, Rev. Dr. Kearney on Manures and Rev. Dr. Jackson on Ploughing and Harrowing. Bogs seemed to hold a particular interest for bishops. Archbishop King wrote a treatise on the "Bogs and Loughs of Ireland" while Theophilus Bolton, Archbishop of Cashel, "was an improver of land by draining large and useless bogs, and turning them into pasture and tillage".[10] Other papers were read on topics ranging from lead, copper and coal to bee-keeping.

The question of applying for a Royal Charter was addressed at one of the February meetings and a copy of the Royal Society's Charter was ordered to be procured as a precedent. This was an issue to be taken on by Prior and others in the years ahead. Dr. Stephens presented the Society with a manuscript of Sir William Petty later in the year. A number of new ploughs were imported and members were invited to attend a special trial of them in the Phoenix Park. Because of the number of meetings, problems occasionally arose on accommodation at the Parliament House and some were held at Anne's Coffee Shop in Dame Street, while Mr. Gunn's bookshop in Capel Street provided an accommodation address.

Prior and other members were commissioned to find a tract of land suitable for a nursery, a task, like so many others in the early years, which fell to Prior. He found a small piece of ground which he liked at Ballybough Bridge and the site was presented to the Society by a Mr. Everard for three years free of rent and thereafter at £6 an acre. Here the Society's first experiments in hop growing got under way. This was a feather in Prior's cap and a significant milestone in the growth of the Society. In the Spring of 1733, two thousand four hundred "hop sets" were planted and also four hundred "cyder trees". The plot at Ballybough

Bridge proved ideal for early experiments in plant growing but as activities increased it soon became evident that more ground was needed. In 1736 the Society leased four acres of land and a house near Martin's Lane, Marlborough Street, for 61 years at £24 per annum.

The Society made its first appearance in the public press in *Pue's Occurrences* of 24 February, 1733, with a notice as to its intentions of publishing instructions in Husbandry from time to time. The notice read:

"The Dublin Society, intending to publish instruction in several branches of Husbandry, desire gentlemen and farmers in the country will be pleased to communicate to the Society any useful improvement they know or practice in any part of husbandry, by letter directed to Anthony Sheppard, jun., Esq. in Dublin. And whereas it has been found upon frequent trials, that the new invented plow, lately brought from England, plows lay and stubble ground very well with half the number of cattle required for the common plow, when it is managed by a plowman who knows the right way of using it, but has sometimes not answered expectation from lack of skill in the person who held it. This is to give notice that if gentlemen who have got the new plow, will send their plowmen to Dublin, and direct them to Mr. Thomas Prior, at Mr. Gunn's, bookseller in Capel St., care shall be taken to have them instructed *gratis*, in two or three days at most, the right way of using the said plow, by persons well skilled, who live near Dublin." The plough referred to was the invention of Jethro Tull which Prior had purchased for the Society for the sum of £10 16s 8d.

From the early days of the Dublin Society Prior ensured that information on best farming methods was circulated to landowners so that they could improve their output. Pamphlets were published and circulated on various farming topics. The introduction of Tull's plough was the first practical attempt in providing skilled instruction on an important farming activity. It marked the start of the vital role the Society would play in advising and instructing in farming and related activities in the years and decades ahead. It was this response to practical needs, with a particular emphasis on progress and development, which would be the key to the Society's success.

References

(1) *Thomas Prior (1681-1751)* by Desmond Clarke. Dublin. 1951.
(2) *The Story of the Royal Dublin Society* by Terence de Vere White. Tralee. 1955.

THOMAS PRIOR

(3) Prior's treatise *Instructions for Planting and Managing Hops* was later used in full in Mill's major work, *System of Practical Husbandry*, published in 1767 prefaced with the comment: "The best method yet laid down for the culture of hops is delivered to the following effect in a pamphlet drawn up by and published by order of the respectable Dublin Society. Meenan and Clarke note in *The Royal Dublin Society 1731-1981* that "this was written more than thirty years after the Society has issued the pamphlet and when hop growing was common in the south of England. In recent times this pamphlet has been consulted despite modern advances in hop cultivation and harvesting."

(4) "It is a little difficult to define Prior's position vis-a-vis Berkeley, though there is a lot to be said for the comprehensive description that he was Berkeley's *alter ego*." Extract from *Thomas Prior (1681-1751)* by Desmond Clarke.

(5) As (2)

(6) As (1).

(7) ibid.

(8) *A History of The Royal Dublin Society* by Henry F. Berry. London. 1915.

(9) ibid.

(10) ibid.

CHAPTER 5

Early Challenges

A fter the initial flurry of activity, Prior and his colleagues experienced difficulties in the dissemination of information so vital for further progress. In 1736 they once again resorted to the press, this time by publishing weekly articles in the *Dublin Newsletter* on useful agricultural topics. These papers covered a wide variety of subjects and appealed not only to the large landowner but also the small and medium farmer. An extra five hundred copies of each article were distributed throughout the country. One notice inserted in the *Dublin Newsletter* reads: "Such gentlemen who live in the country and are not already supplied with this paper, and who are willing to encourage so useful a work are desired to send notice thereof by the beginning of January next, and they shall constantly be supplied with same; also with the best collection of news both foreign and domestic."

The Phoenix Park was a favourite location for ploughing and similar demonstrations. Public activities there were largely restricted until Lord Chesterfield became Lord Lieutenant. The Park had been formed in 1662 when the lands surrounding the Viceregal residence were acquired for a deer park. Chesterfield had shrubs planted and gravel paths laid and, in line with his tolerant policy and amiable disposition, popularised it as a recreation centre for Dubliners and visitors.[1] Demonstrations were, on occasions, held at other locations in Dublin and in various parts of the country. Prior and other members of the Society travelled to various farms to inspect newly invented or improved implements.[2]

The problem of the scarcity of coin, and small coin in particular, persisted long after the Wood's halfpence controversy of the 1720s. Prior had shown a keen interest in the subject and it was most likely on his prompting that the Society in 1735 asked himself and some other members to draw the heads for a treatise "upon the present state of the Coin in this kingdom, and the inconvenience to the trade and manufacture thereof from want of small coin and of any schemes to prevent this".

There is no record of the treatise being completed though Prior, in a letter, urged the Government to set up an Irish mint and issue gold and silver coin bearing parity with English coinage, instead of being debased to the enrichment of mint officials. The reason why the paper was not finalised was, most likely, because Prior's close friend and confidant, Berkeley, now the Bishop of Cloyne, focused on the issues of coinage and the establishment of an Irish mint in the first part of his *Querist*, which was published in 1735.

Hone and Rossi pictured the new Bishop of Cloyne as a tired, disillusioned and fast-ageing man whose "wish … brought him to the extreme south of the island … He, who in the first years of his existence, had proposed to hold the country high before the eyes of the world – who had felt himself as an Irishman first and foremost – had too long forgotten his native country and even his duties in it. Now, at last, he returned: perhaps the man who had dreamed to conquer the world with his philosophy or his American dream, and sought with humble heart his brothers in penury, the land that has the destiny of being forgotten as soon as possible – by its sons and by its foes."[3]

Berkeley was far from being a spent force during his time in Cloyne. Apart from his philosophical writings he immersed himself in the social and economic problems of his diocese. He also introduced an appreciation of the finer things in life. "In the episcopal palace of Cloyne (wrote Dr. Smith) the eye was entertained with a great variety of good paintings, as well as the ear with concerts of excellent music. There were here some pieces of the best masters: as a Magdalen by Rubens; besides several good paintings performed in the house. The example had the effect of creating a spirit of emulation among the neighbouring gentry."[4]

But his Cloyne retreat was hardly a haven of bliss and mellow fruitfulness. One of the longest and most severe economic depressions in history due to the destruction of the Irish export trade in woollen goods and the recurrent failure of the potato crop had reduced the lot of the majority to a miserable existence. Conditions in the south were particularly bad because of the lack of an industrial base. Berkeley was exasperated by the distress that surrounded him and, with the help of Prior, he tried to relieve the hardships of local people by creating employment and performing good works.

As Johnston writes: "Famine was frequent, and epidemics of disease frequently raged in the country. Berkeley considered that it was not inconsistent with his pastoral duties to labour for the material welfare of all those (the vast majority of whom were Roman Catholics) among whom his lot was cast. In the most literal sense he followed in the footsteps of the Master and 'went about doing good', caring for the bodies of all, as well as for the souls of those committed to his charge. … It was no mere accident that Berkeley concentrated his attention on problems of social economics from the moment when he found himself plunged in the environment of his rustic diocese."[5]

His *Querist*, first published in 1735, was directed at his own country-men as well as the decision-makers in Dublin and London. In it he posed practical questions and sought practical answers. Johnston writes: "He wanted to make them understand the true nature of the evils which all right-minded men deplored, and to realise with him how easily they might be remedied; he believed that if he could only persuade men to see the essential nature of these problems, as he saw it, the application of the necessary public and private remedies would follow as a matter of course."[6]

Prior was a major influence on Berkeley's economic reasoning and this is reflected in *The Querist*. Both men consulted closely on the issues raised in the pamphlet. Berkeley argues that Ireland's future prosperity would be achieved through internal solutions, by developing trade at home and by the establishment of a national bank, conclusions strongly supported by Prior. Prior with Madden's assistance arranged for the pub-lication of the Dublin edition while Sir John Percival looked after the London publication. Because Prior was so closely associated with the Dublin Society it may be assumed that his economic theories closely reflected prevailing thinking of members and the interests and concerns of the Dublin Society can readily be identified in the pamphlet. Its pub-lication boosted the efforts of Society members to stimulate the indus-trial life of the country and to introduce modern methods into farming.

Parts Two and Three of *The Querist* were published in the succeeding years. In further editions some questions are dropped and others added. One question omitted in later editions related to the proposal for a national bank. Berkeley, on his only extended absence from Cloyne, went to Dublin to promote the plan, but his efforts failed. Noting the omission, he wrote "it may be time enough to take again in hand when the public shall deem disposed to make use of such an expedient". While the earlier editions were published anonymously, he did allow his name to be used in later publications: "I had determined myself never to pre-fix my name to *The Querist*, but in the last edition was overruled by a friend, who was remarkable for pursuing the public interest with as much diligence as others do their own. I apprehend the same censure on this that I incurred upon another occasion, for meddling out of my profes-sion; though to feed the hungry and clothe the naked, by promoting an honest industry, will, perhaps, be deemed no improper employment for a clergyman who still thinks himself a member of the commonwealth. As the sum of human happiness is supposed to consist in the goods of mind, body, and fortune, I would fain make my studies of some use to mankind with regard to each of these three particulars, and hope it will not be thought faulty or indecent in any man, of what profession soever, to offer his mite towards improving the manners, health, and prosperity of his fellow-creatures." The friend to whom Berkeley refers was almost certainly Prior.

Berkeley achieved what he set out to do with his *Querist* which was to encourage his fellow-countrymen to think. Lecky asserted that the work "is in itself sufficient to give him a place among the great economists of his age". Hone and Rossi noted that "this economic tract, it has been observed with some truth, marked the first occasion on which a leading Irishman had openly avowed his love for all his countrymen". One of Berkeley's queries was added in support of the point raised: "whether it be not vain to project the prosperity of the Protestant landowners and manufacturers and not take account of the vast body of the people".

The Dublin Society grew in membership and prestige. A list of members published in 1734 contained 267 names including 12 bishops, 16 peers, 5 judges and a number of Members of the Irish Parliament, including the Chancellor of the Exchequer and the Speaker. It would appear, however, that as the Society's first decade passed by a number of these were members in name only and were neither paying subscriptions nor playing an active role in the Society.[7]

A series of recommendations was drawn up to streamline the running of the Society. Membership was limited to one hundred active members and a standing committee was appointed for the general government of the Society; four other committees were formed for specific purposes, namely correspondence, experiment, publications and accounts. This arrangement marked the beginning of the committee system which has governed the Society to the present day.[8] Prior was a member of all the committees except accounts, though even here he countersigned the accounts fortnightly.

The Society wielded considerable influence but its work was hampered by a lack of funds. Enter Dr. Samuel Madden, a Church of Ireland clergyman and well-to-do landowner of Manor Waterhouse in County Fermanagh. His mother was a sister of William and Sir Thomas Molyneux. Though often designated as a founder of the Society, sometimes as in Lecky's History of the Eighteenth Century he is credited with sharing the honour with Prior, de Vere White emphasises that "he, in fact, was never a member".[9] Clarke, however, notes in his work on Thomas Prior that he became a member in 1733. He was certainly its first patron and his financial support, in the form of premiums, benefited the Society greatly at a time when it was most needed. The premium schemes he initiated continued to help foster the aims of the Society long after he was dead. In 1738 he published his *Reflections and Resolutions Proper for the Gentlemen of Ireland*, a work which Meenan and Clarke praised as "containing many admirable suggestions more or less in accord with the aims and objects of the Society".[10] De Vere White has a different version of Madden's literary contributions: "Madden's writings are devoid of originality. The ideas are stolen from Dobbs, Prior and Berkeley." He depicts the man consigned to history as "Premium" Madden as a henpecked man, "with more energy than talent, he enjoyed a synthetic fame by judicious employment of his patronage and purse". De Vere White has other amusing if unadmiring things to say about the man but it is his reference to Madden's bust that is a real gem. He writes: "The Doctor's bust in marble in the Society's premises at Balls Bridge reveals a fat, satisfied face, eloquent of self-importance, but devoid of sensitivity. How poorly the head compares with Prior's beside it in the passage."[11]

Whatever his shortcomings, Madden held Prior in high regard and there was a strong bond of friendship between them. In his *Reflections* Madden refers to Prior "as worthy and as useful a Member of his country as I know in it." His thinking on the evils of absenteeism corresponded directly with Prior's rationale on the issue. Like Prior he admired and praised the stay-at-home landlord. He wrote: "A gentleman who lives on his estate and spends a large share of his rents there, does not only, like a giant tree, necessarily improve the soil it grows on by the leaves and most that falls from it; but by the warmth, and shade, and shelter which it casts around." In 1739 he penned anonymously his *Letter to the Dublin Society on the improving of their Fund* which dealt with means of boosting the Society's income and the purpose to which the increased funds might best be applied. Madden suggested that funds should be sought from persons of fortune and that the Society should seek incorporation by Royal Charter. The funds should be devoted to the encouragement of manufactures; and experimental farms should be started to study the husbandry best suited to the country. He concluded with an offer of £130 a year for two years and undertook to continue it for life when £500 was procured, "provided the Society apply his little fund to the views they are directed to with their usual activity and prudence".

Madden could soon reveal that he had obtained subscriptions of nearly £900 per annum for promoting arts and manufactures. On

14 February he was asked to leave the subscription roll with Prior. The premiums were advertised and a full list was published a little later.

The Society was revitalised by Madden's scheme. Webb in his *Compendium of Irish Biography* writes, "while Thomas Prior was most active in founding the Society, Madden was one of those to whom the ultimate success of this great national institution was due". The premium adjudicators, of whom Prior was the most involved, met each week, either in the city market, Anne's Coffee Shop or the Parliament House to judge and award premiums. Even de Vere White somewhat grudgingly admits that Madden's intervention was vital to the Society's future: "Whatever the merits of his system, Madden provided exactly what the Society required at the time; he introduced a dramatic note to proceedings."

The list of premiums expanded with the years. There was no project too big or too small that could qualify. The scheme rewarded every area of human activity in industry, agriculture and the arts. A number of new paper mills were established, new inventions were tested, implements tried out and raw material sourced. There were premiums awarded for the killing of rats and the city of Kilkenny won a £10 premium for clearing its streets of beggars by finding employment for them. Prior immersed himself in the Society's activities which, as Clarke writes: "even in the first ten years of (its) existence … was performing voluntarily the functions of present day state departments. … we must not lose sight of the fact that it was from the small beginnings, fostered with pioneering zeal by Prior and his associates, that most of our national institutions and at least one state department sprang. Few realise today that the National Library, Museum and Art Gallery, Botanic Gardens, Veterinary College, School of Art, College of Science and Department of Agriculture were at one time part of the Society, either initiated by or entrusted to its care. In founding and establishing the Dublin Society, Prior and his associates created and instilled a spirit of self-reliance and independence in the more nationally-minded and public-spirited Anglo-Irish, and developed a system of voluntary and unselfish service which has marked the manifold activities of the Royal Dublin Society for more than two centuries."[12]

Apart from premiums, Madden had a second string to his plan for survival of the Royal Society – a Royal Charter. If de Vere White gives a somewhat grudging credit to Madden for introducing premiums, he does not feel he should be credited with either coming up with the idea initially or the procurement of a Royal Charter for the Society, which distinction was finally achieved in 1750: "Madden is usually given the credit for having through his influence obtained the Charter for the Society, but (Lord) Chesterfield was in correspondence with Prior on the subject (previously), and promised to get one if Prior and others who, I am sure, mean well, and can judge well, think upon the whole that a Charter would be beneficial".[13]

References

(1) *Encyclopaedia of Dublin* by Douglas Bennett. Dublin, 1991.
(2) *The Royal Dublin Society 1731-1981* edited by James Meenan and Desmond Clarke. Dublin. 1981.
(3) *Life of George Berkeley* by J. Hone and N. Rossi. 1938.
(4) ibid.
(5) *Bishop Berkeley's Querist in Historical Perspective* by Joseph Johnston. Dundalk. 1970.
(6) ibid.
(7) As (2).
(8) ibid.
(9) *The Story of the Royal Dublin Society* by Terence de Vere White. Tralee. 1955.
(10) As (2).
(11) As (9).
(12) *Thomas Prior (1781-1851)* by Desmond Clarke. Dublin. 1951.
(13) As (9).

CHAPTER 6

Tar-Water, Mosse and Chesterfield

The close bond between Berkeley and Prior continued throughout their lives. There was regular correspondence keeping each in touch with the other's thoughts and troubles. Prior made a yearly trip to Cloyne and he was always received with open arms by the Bishop and his family. They looked forward to his annual visit and encouraged him to come more often.

Famine swept the land in 1739, 1740 and 1741 and plague caused havoc in its wake. One sixth of the population of the country had died as a result of the catastrophic potato famine of 1739 alone. Berkeley wrote to Prior informing him of the "endless distress of the sick and the poor" in the Cork area. Failing to find a remedy to cure the pestilence from any other source, the Bishop looked to his own devices. He began the study of diseases on scientific lines, and he solicited Prior's help in seeking out books on medicine which he was to send to Cloyne.

Berkeley was at his wit's end to find a remedy. On 8 February, 1741, he wrote informing Prior that he had found a cure. By administering "a heaped spoonful of a roisin powdered fine in a little broth" he had cured dysentery, he claimed. A little time later he informed Prior of his belief that tar-water might be useful as a preventative or a cure. He also stated that he had tried a cure proposed by Prior involving the use of briar roots, but without success.

Berkeley became obsessed with finding a cure and with further trials he became more and more convinced that he had found a panacea in tar-water. In 1744 he published a book on the subject, *A Chain of Philosophical Reflexions and Inquiries concerning the Virtues of Tar-Water*, better known as *Siris*. It was an instant success. People bought the book and tar-water was soon in big demand. The work opens with observations on the medicinal values of tar-water. Item number 21 is an example of Berkeley's belief in its curative qualities: "Tar Water is extremely pectoral and restorative, and if I am to judge, from what experience I have had, it possesseth the most valuable qualities ascribed to the several balsams of Peru, of Capivi and even to the balm of Gilead, such is the virtue in asthmas and pleurisies, in obstructions and ulcerous erosions of the inward parts. Balsams as hath been already observed are apt to offend the stomach. For the strengthening whereof it is the best medicine I have ever tried." The book runs to 261 pages containing 368 observations in all. After giving the full tribute to tar-water the work rambles into a discussion on the metaphysical natures of the physical and spiritual universe as well as God.

This was new ground for the Bishop. He had already trodden on toes in the past with his political and economic theories. Now it was the turn of the medical profession to get alarmed. The book was denounced by physicians and a great debate ensued: "Pamphlets of attack and defence fell from the printing presses in increasing numbers."[1] Prior got caught up in the controversy. He staunchly defended his friend. The renowned Trinity historian, A. A. Luce commented: "His (Berkeley) Dublin friends, Prior and Faulkner, stood by him through thick and thin. Prior, was, of course, acting in an unofficial capacity, but he was secretary of the Dublin Society, and his public actions at this juncture in connection with public health were so strong and striking that, we may be sure, they must have been in general accord with the policy of the body he represented." Prior wrote several letters to the *Dublin Journal* and *The Gentleman's Magazine* in defence of tar-water, citing numerous cures which had been brought to his attention. Berkeley in returning the support given by his friend addressed two *Open Letters to T... P... Esq., from the Author of Siris, containing some farther Remarks on the Virtues of Tar-Water and the Methods of Preparing and using of it.* The controversy waged on. Prior appealed through the press for information about cures and benefits and he got a good response. This resulted in the publication by Prior in 1746 of *An Authentick Narrative of the Success of Tar-Water.* As Clarke comments: "It has no literary qualities, nor does it claim any; it is typical of Prior, bare facts in defence of Berkeley, and incidentally of a book (*Siris*) which today is recognised, not for its advocacy of Tar-Water, but as one of Berkeley's greatest works, 'the unstudied murmurings of a cultured and persuasive philosopher who in the evening of his life has fallen a-musing'."[2]

Prior's interest in public health was not confined to the promotion of the curative qualities of tar-water and in its dispensation to the disease-ridden masses. He also gave valuable support to Bartholomew Mosse in establishing the first maternity hospital in these islands. The population of Dublin was expanding rapidly in the 1740s. A series of potato famines had forced poor families in the country to seek relief in Dublin: "This new wave of immigrants to the city were wretchedly poor; they crawled

Thomas Prior (from a mezzotint by Charles Spooner).

up to Dublin – sometimes literally on their hands and knees".[3] Childbirth facilities were absolutely appalling and poor expectant mothers were exposed to horrific conditions and lack of professional care: "Their lodgings were generally in cold garrets open to every wind, or in damp cellars subject to floods from excessive rains, destitute of attendance, medicines, and often of proper food."[4] Mosse, like Prior, was born in the Queen's County (now County Laois). He was son of the Rector of Maryborough (now Portlaoise) and grandson of the chaplain to William III in Ireland in the Jacobite War. After developing an interest in midwifery while on a military assignment in Europe during the wars of the Spanish Succession, he was determined on his return to Ireland to improve childbirth conditions here. Browne observes: "We can only assume that Mosse must have been moved and upset by the plight of Dublin women as they bore their children, and it was perhaps his concern about this matter that stirred his imagination to dream about a maternity hospital, to provide food, shelter and medical care for women in their hour of need."[5]

The Mosse family were well respected among "persons of wealth and influence" and although man-midwives were looked down upon by the medical profession, Bartholomew, was well established and admired as a surgeon and did not, as a result, suffer from popular prejudices of his medical speciality. Mosse sought support from whatever person or source he could get it. By 1743 he had on board a number of patrons committed to helping him found a lying-in hospital. One important friend and ally was Richard Cassells (Castle), among the most famous architects of his or any age. His name is associated with Carton, Russborough and with Leinster House. Gilbert, in his *History of the City of Dublin*, noted the friendship of Mosse and Cassells: "Cassells … when in Dublin passed his evenings with Dr. Mosse of the hospital, and a few more musical friends, at a tavern where they seldom left before three or four o'clock in the morning." Cassells is thought to have drawn up the plans for the Rotunda free of charge because of his friendship and esteem for Mosse. Both men would later become members of the Dublin Society.

Indeed many of Mosse's friends had strong connections with the Society. These included Robert Clayton, Bishop of Clogher, a wealthy and benevolent divine who fell from grace for holding heretical views and Dr. Patrick Delany, the Dean of Down, whose donation to Mosse's project is the first recorded. He was reported in *Pue's Occurrences* of 27 March 1743 to have subscribed four guineas a year. Thomas Prior is also noted as one of Mosse's early supporters.[6] Mosse secured a house in George's Lane, off South Great George's Street, and mustered a small team for its management. This group, later to become directors, included Prior as well as the Reverend Dr. Wynne, his co-secretary at the Dublin Society.

The first lying-in hospital was opened on 15 March 1745. It had only a few beds and the building and facilities were far from ideal but, for Mosse and his associates, it was a start. Mosse's priority was to raise funds for the day-to-day running of the hospital and his driving ambition was to provide the best possible facilities for all who needed them. He received disappointing support from his profession but he proved an accomplished fund-raiser with Prior and others behind him all the way. Mosse promoted drama and music events which were well-attended and the purse-strings loosened. Dublin hosted the first performance of Handel's *Messiah* in 1742 and the proceeds went to Mercer's Hospital and the Charitable Infirmary. Taking the cue from this venture, Mosse staged a number of Handel's works to further his own project, including a performance of *Esther* in 1746, which was attended by an audience of 500 people including the Lord Lieutenant, Lord Chesterfield. Though he remained in office for a mere eight months, Chesterfield distinguished himself as a wise and caring benefactor, a man with the utmost regard for Thomas Prior and the work of the Dublin Society. Mosse and his directors in 1748 acquired a four acre site, where the Rotunda now stands. In order to help finances, part of the plot was laid out as a leisure park on the plan of the Vauxhall Gardens in London. The success of this undertaking and the lotteries he ran for the hospital project rebounded on him, however. He was openly accused of embezzlement and had to flee the country. He was even imprisoned for a short time – not a pleasant prospect in the mid-eighteenth century. However, he escaped, hid in the Welsh mountains for a while and, on his return, was able to vindicate himself to all concerned.[7] Although there are no records to indicate the role he played, it is apparent from the nature of the man, who stood by his friends, such as in Berkeley's case, that Prior stood firmly by his friend Mosse in his darkest hour. This is supported by "the fact that the latter perfected a deed of trust in 1750, in which he declared that the ground was taken by him for and only for 'the poor distressed lying-in women' and he named as trustees with himself the Rev. George Leslie, Doctor of Divinity, Thomas Prior and Ralph Simpson. Certainly a tribute to Prior who at the time was an old man."[8] The foundation stone for the new hospital was laid on 4 June 1751 by the Lord Mayor of Dublin "and the greatest appearance of nobility and gentry assembled" to join in the festivities.[9] Prior, now aged seventy, had fallen into poor health by this time and would die before the year's end.

Chesterfield, unusual if not unique amongst the English administrators, had not only a good knowledge of the Ireland of his time, but had a caring concern for the country and its people. Lecky sums up the brief but effective Chesterfield appointment: "Though it unfortunately only lasted for eight months (it) was eminently successful. He came over in the beginning of the rebellion of 1745, and the care with which he watched over the material prosperity of the country, the happy ridicule with which he discouraged the rumours of Popish risings, the firmness with which he refused to follow the precedent of 1715, when all Catholic chapels were closed during the rebellion, the unusual public spirit with which he administered his patronage, and the tact he invariably exhibited during the critical circumstances of the time, made his government one of the most remarkable in Irish history." Lecky attributed Chesterfield's enlightened approach as being probably the reason "for the tranquillity of Ireland at a time when England and Scotland were torn by civil war". While Chesterfield's policy of appeasement to Roman Catholics was responsible in some degree for the peace that prevailed, a more potent reason for Ireland's tranquillity was the sheer destitution of the native Irish and the suppression they had endured for the previous fifty years. Chesterfield knew from his own system of intelligence-gathering that the old Irish had not the appetite for another war. He knew that the fight had been finally beaten out of them in the bitter wars of conquest of the 17th century. Talk persisted, however, of a growing belligerence amongst the native Irish. The rumours were doing the rounds in fashionable Dublin circles but Chesterfield was dismissive of the threat. One morning a courtier burst into his apartment, while he was sipping chocolate in bed, with the startling news that "the Papists were rising" in Connaught. "Ah", said Chesterfield, looking at his watch, "'tis nine o'clock; time for them to rise". Far from complying to ascendancy demands, as other viceroys had invariably done, and would do again, Chesterfield, instead of raising new regiments to defend the settlers, sent four battalions of soldiers then in Ireland to reinforce the Duke of Cumberland's civil war campaign on the other side of the Irish Sea.

Chesterfield was shocked by an incident that occurred at a clandestine Mass-house in Dublin after his arrival as viceroy. O'Hanlon recounts the terrible tragedy: "A number of persons were assembled by stealth in an upper room of a house in Dublin to hear Mass, when suddenly the floor gave way, and they were all precipitated into the room beneath. Ten were killed, including the priest, and many were seriously injured."[10] Chesterfield immediately put a stop to priest-hunting and ordered a relaxation of the penal laws. On 8 October, 1745, he addressed

Parliament and "greatly disgusted the fierce and gloomy bigots of the Ascendancy" by making it clear that active persecution of the penal code was to be suspended although, as Mitchel reminds us that "indulgence was contrary to law".[11] Chesterfield allowed Catholic chapels to be reopened and Catholic clergy to carry out their pastoral duties without the customary harassment from the authorities. The overly zealous magistrates who had earned distinction by active prosecution of Papists under former viceroys now found only discouragement and rebuke at the Castle. Chancellors, judges, and sheriffs were made to understand that to do the King's business 'they must leave the common enemy in peace for the present'.[12]

Despite Chesterfield's dismissal of any Irish rebellion, the Jacobite revolt in Scotland caused an anxiety amongst the settlers that the sons and grandsons of the dispossessed might think the time appropriate to make a move to reclaim lost possessions. Berkeley cooperated with Chesterfield's conciliatory policy. He apparently sensed "a latent spirit of Jacobitism" and feared that the native Irish might be secretly plotting a revolt which caused him to write a *Letter to the Roman Catholics of Cloyne*. In a kind and paternal way, he exhorted them to keep the peace and to attend quietly to their own industry. What guarantee was there, he asked, that a Stuart King would restore the land of Ireland to its original owners? Charles II and James II had been deceivers of the Irish. The Pretender, if he succeeded, would no doubt seize Protestant estates; but these would be the reward of 'his foreign favourites', Berkeley warned. Mitchel was not impressed by this action of a man he otherwise respected: "The Bishop is evidently at a loss for arguments which he can urge upon this proscribed, disfranchised race, why they should take their lot quietly and be loyal to a Government that does not recognize their existence."[13]

We can take it that Berkeley had the welfare of the Catholics as well as the Protestants of Cloyne at heart when penning this remarkable letter. He knew that violence would have been met with violence and all the commendable liberalising policies introduced by Chesterfield would unravel in such an event. Berkeley also addressed a letter to the Catholic clergy who responded favourably to "this unprecedented gesture coming from an Anglican Bishop of the period".[14] They publicly commended him as "the good man, the polite gentleman and the true patriot". Circular letters were sent to the parish priests of the Dublin diocese recommending the "zealous execution" of the matter of Berkeley's address. Berkeley saw in Chesterfield a friend; so too did Prior, Madden, Faulkner and the other liberals of the Ascendancy class. Berkeley instructed Prior to obtain 'a fine copy' of *The Querist* for presentation to the new viceroy, and to underline the entries in advocacy of a National Bank. Prior and members of the Dublin Society presented an address to Chesterfield and invited him to become President of the Society. Chesterfield warmed to Prior from his early days in Dublin and admitted great admiration for him. "I know few people," he wrote, "who, like you, employ both their time and their fortunes in doing public good, without the thoughts or expectation of private advantage; when I say advantage, I mean it in the common acceptance of the word, which, thanks to the virtue of our times, implies only money, for otherwise your advantage is very considerable, from the consciousness of the good you do – the greatest advantage which an honest mind is capable of enjoying." He also reminded Prior to "think of your manufactures at least as much as of your militia, and be as much upon your guard against Poverty as against Popery; take my word for it, you are more in danger of the former than of the latter".

Prior kept Chesterfield updated on the work of the Society, which impressed the viceroy greatly, sufficiently indeed for him to ask the Prime Minister, the Duke of Newcastle, to support his appeal for a Royal bounty. In a letter to the Prime Minister, Chesterfield wrote: "The Dublin Society is really a very useful establishment. It consists of many considerable people, and has been kept up hitherto by voluntary subscriptions. They give premiums for the improvement of lands, for plantations, for manufactures. They furnish many materials for those improvements in the poorer and less cultivated parts of the kingdom, and have certainly done a great deal of good. The bounty they apply for to his Majesty is £500 a year, which, in my humble opinion, would be properly bestowed." A few months later Prior reported that Lord Chesterfield had shown him the King's letter granting £500 per annum during his pleasure, to be laid out as the Society thought fit. The Royal letter, signed by Pelham, Fox and Arundell, was transmitted to the Society on 8 May, 1746. Chesterfield's support for the Dublin Society enhanced its progress. He was enthusiastic about plans submitted by Prior for the establishment of an academy or drawing school. This led to youths receiving art instruction at Robert West's Academy in George's Lane and others being apprenticed with the noted sculptor, John van Nost. An art school was established in 1756, five years after Prior's death, at Shaw's Court, off Dame Street, which marked the beginning of an illustrious involvement by the Society in the artistic life of the country.

Chesterfield was recalled after eight months much to the relief of the administration and ascendancy hardliners who did not trust him. But his recall after such a short stay must have come as a bitter disappointment to Prior and his associates. Chesterfield maintained a keen interest in Ireland's progress and corresponded regularly with Prior, Madden and others with whom he had become acquainted when in Ireland. Prior and Madden jointly pursued the prospect of a Royal Charter for the Dublin Society. In a letter to Madden, Chesterfield expressed reservations as to the benefits such a conferral might have on the Society. "I see many advantages that might arise from it", he wrote. "But I must at the same time own that I foresee some dangers too. Jobs have hitherto always accompanied Charters, however they may have been calculated to prevent them. The Dublin Society has hitherto gone on excellently well, and done infinite good: why? because, that not being a permanent, incorporated Society, and having no employments to dispose of, and depending only for its existence on their own good behaviour, it was not a theatre for Jobbers to show their skill upon; but when once established by Charter the very advantages which are expected from, and which, I believe, will attend that Charter, I fear may prove fatal. It may become an object of party, and Parliamentary views (for you know how low they stoop); in which case it will become subservient to the worst instead of the best designs. Remember the Linen Board where the paltry dividend of a little flax seed was become the seed of jobs, which indeed produced one hundred fold." Chesterfield also warned of the lethal mixture of money and drink: "jobs and claret engross and ruin the people of fashion, and the ordinary people (as is usual in every country) imitate them in little monetary and mistaken views of present profit, and in whiskey".

While Prior's letters to Chesterfield are typically to the point and generally concern themselves with Royal Society business, Madden's letters to him mixed business with pleasure. As well as mentioning premiums and a Charter they also contain samples of his poetry which he hoped might impress the good Lord. In his letters to Madden, Chesterfield almost invariably sends greetings to Prior and in his letters to Prior, he sends greetings to Berkeley. He wrote congratulating Madden for nurturing the spirit of industry in the country "all of which, I may venture to say, is originally owing to your judicious and indefatigable endeavours for the good of your country. You know the nature of mankind in general and the nature of our countrymen in particular (for I still think and call myself an Irishman) well enough to know that the invitation by premiums would be much more effectual than laws, or remote considerations of public good. … The Dublin Society, and, in particular, my good friends, the Bishop of Meath and Prior, have seconded you very well, and it is not saying too much of them to say that they deserve better of

Ireland than any one other set of men in it; I will not even except the Parliament."

Prior sent him samples of fine writing and printing paper which was being newly manufactured in Ireland. Chesterfield suggested other products that might be successfully manufactured in Ireland, including the making of glass bottles. He advised Prior that premiums should be given without publishing them so as "not to alarm our glass people here". As for glass manufacture, he commented: "I wish every man in Ireland were obliged to make as many bottles as he empties, and your manufacture would be a flourishing one indeed", proceeding to condemn the drink abuse among the ruling class. "I still less recant what I said about claret, which is known and melancholy truth, and I could add a great deal more upon that subject. ... I believe that you will allow that the Claret Board, if there were one, would be much better attended than the Linen Board, unless when flax-seed was distributed. I am sensible that I shall be reckoned a very shallow politician, for my attention to such trifling objects, as the improvement of your lands, the extension of your manufactures, and the increase of your trade, which only tend to the advantage of the public, whereas an able Lord Lieutenant ought to employ his thoughts in greater matters. He should think of jobs for parasites, sops for enemies, managing parties, and engaging Parliaments to vote away their own and their fellow subjects' liberties and properties. But these great arts of Government, I confess, are above me, and people should not go out of their depth. I will modestly be content with wishing Ireland all the good that is possible, and with doing it all the good that I can; and so weak am I that I would rather be distinguished and remembered by the name of the Irish Lord Lieutenant than by that of the Lord Lieutenant of Ireland". While Chesterfield's letters to Madden all acknowledge receipt of the clergyman's cantos, in his letters to Prior his acknowledgements are usually for samples of manufactures and the occasional small gift, such as snuff, sent to him. Chesterfield forwarded a "large donation"[15] to Prior for the use of the Dublin Society which he again compliments in the accompanying letter: "They have done more good for Ireland, with regards to the arts and industry, than all the laws that could have been formed; for, unfortunately, there is a perverseness in our natures which prompts us to resist authority, though otherwise inclined enough to do the thing, if left to our own choice. Invitation, example and fashion, with some premiums attending them, are, I am convinced, the only method of bringing people in Ireland to do what they ought to do; and that is the plan of your Society."

Despite his reservations, Chesterfield supported the Society's bid for the royal imprimatur and on 2 April 1750 his work on behalf of the Society was crowned by the granting of a Charter under the seal of King George II. Thirty-two members were named in the Charter including Lord Chesterfield. De Vere White notes that Madden's name does not appear in the list and that he was not subsequently elected. He concedes, however, that "the amount he awarded in premiums discounts the least suggestion that he grudged the modest annual subscription". For Prior, the granting of the Royal Charter was the ultimate acknowledgement of his tireless and inspired work on behalf of the Society for many years. It was also the last great milestone in the Society's development that he would live to see.

References

(1) *Thomas Prior (1681-1751)* by Desmond Clarke. Dublin. 1951.
(2) ibid.
(3) *Masters, Midwives and Ladies-in-Waiting: The Rotunda Hospital 1745-1995* edited by Alan Browne. Dublin. 1995.
(4) *Book of the Rotunda Hospital* by T.P.C. Kirkpatrick and H. Jellett. London. 1913.
(5) *The Story of the Rotunda Hospital* by Alan D. H. Browne.
(6) As (3).
(7) As (5).
(8) As (1).
(9) As (3).
(10) *History of the Queen's County* by J. Canon O'Hanlon and E. O'Leary. Dublin. 1914.
(11) *The History of Ireland* by John Mitchel.
(12) ibid.
(13) ibid.
(14) *Life of George Berkeley* by J. Hone and N. Rossi. 1938.
(15) As (1).

CHAPTER 7

Final Years

T homas Prior's heavy workload did not decrease with advancing years. The activities of the Dublin Society became more demanding with the success of the premium scheme. He remained in charge of Berkeley's business affairs and his work as Dublin agent for country gentlemen as well his own private interests kept him extremely busy into old age. In his latter years he devoted much of his time to the promotion of the growing of flax and the linen industry, a subject close to his heart. He had transformed the wearing of Irish linen scarves into a political statement. They were first worn for the funeral of Speaker William Conolly in 1729 to encourage the wearing of home-produced rather than imported textiles.[1] Among those whom Prior personally assisted in developing the linen industry was Sir Richard Cox of Dunmanway. On 14 March 1749 Prior wrote to Cox asking him to send on an account of the progress of the industry in the Dunmanway area. Cox's letter of reply was published later.[2] It reveals large areas of land covered with flax, and the existence of mills, a spinning school for boys and girls, bleach yards, a market-house and a school all related to the industry. In three years, from 1746 to 1748, more than forty thousand yards of linen were produced. Three hundred people were employed full-time on the newly established industry in the area. Numerous premiums were awarded to the Dunmanway project by the Dublin Society for excellence in various aspects of the operation. Buoyed by the success of the Dunmanway experiment, Prior later that year published a pamphlet on the linen industry, *An Essay to Encourage and Extend the Linen-Manufacture in Ireland by Praemiums and other Means*. In this Prior appealed to the people of Ireland to grow more flax and he issued guidelines on best practices in growing the flax and in the setting up of a linen industry. It is a typical matter-of-fact Prior at work, a man who, according to Clarke, "had little time to waste on puerilities or even niceties of language; he knew what was required for the good of the country and wrote accordingly".

The linen industry prospered in the north but the early success in the development of the industry in the rest of the country was not sustained. Whatever the underlying reasons for its failure in the south, it was certainly not due to any lack of vision or effort on the part of Prior.

Prior found time for an annual visit to the Berkeley family in Cloyne and for the occasional trip to the old stomping ground of his youth in Rathdowney, where he retained an interest in the family estate. He paid a visit, probably his last, to the Berkeleys in the late summer of 1750. Evidence of this appears in a letter from Will Cooley, Warden of Lohort Castle, to the (Second) Earl of Egmont, a life-long friend of Berkeley, dated 4 September 1750 describing the visit.[3] The letter published by Dr. Luce gives the picture of the "Berkeleys, a happy family, complete with their old friend, Tom Prior, setting out for a brief summer holiday at Killarney". The party stayed overnight at Lohort Castle which was on their route. The letter describes how Prior was particularly interested in the oil used to preserve the firearms of Lohort Castle, an oil invented by a Jesuit for the King of France's arsenal. As Clarke comments: "From this letter we get a clear impression of the enquiring and inventive mind of Prior even as an old man". Cooley mentions Prior's interest in coinage: "I must not conclude this letter without acquainting your Lordship that there is a scheme on foot under the management of Mr. Prior for a coinage for the Kingdom". He adds a note of caution: "I should have told you that it was Mr. Prior that brought the light guinea into discredit, and that he warrants in 6 months there will not be one in the nation." Cooley informs Egmont that the party returned some time later except Mr. Prior "who went to visit his estate in County of Limerick". This is the first and only mention of his interest in an estate in Limerick in any papers relating to Prior.

Prior fell into ill-health during the winter that followed. *The Dublin Journal* of 19 January 1751 reported that "Thomas Prior, Esq., who hath been lately indisposed, is perfectly recovered to the joy of his friends and the Public of Ireland". By 14 March he had recovered sufficiently to attend his first meeting of the Dublin Society for some time. He had rarely missed a meeting or an event of the Society in the twenty years since he helped found it. He continued to attend meetings until 15 June, when Clarke opines that "presumably he retired to Rathdowney". A week after the June meeting, he made his will. His health failed again in the autumn of 1751 and he died at Rathdowney on 21 October. The inscription on the tombstone, which was relocated inside the present church beside the graveyard in which he was buried four days later, reads: "Sacred to the memory of Thomas Prior Esq., who spent a long life in unwearied endeavours to promote the welfare of his country. Every manufacture, every branch of husbandry, will declare this truth. Every useful institution will lament its Friend and Benefactor. He died alas! too soon for Ireland. October the 21st, 1751. Aged 70."

Faulkner wrote the obituary for his *Dublin Journal* a few days later: "It can truly be said of him that he was a patriot for his country, having taken most extraordinary pains for the advancement of Trade and Manufactures in this Kingdom, and never declined the most difficult task where the interest of the public was concerned. No man more ready to perform every good and charitable act than he was. No man more strict in his duties towards God, and from whence following his regard to man in endeavouring to point out the only means of their true happiness in the world, by recommending industry for the welfare of their families, and consequently the good of the Community. How much we lament such a loss! A loss that everyone must feel! As a patriot, if not doing his country in General all the service in his power, and never grasping at authority, or looking for a reward, be a virtue in these days, lament the unhappy tidings! As a gentleman he lived elegant but not profuse, always assisting the poor. ... In his fellowship he was sincere and flattery was his aversion. To sum up his character, he had learning without pedantry, charity, benevolence and every good quality without ostentation; honour and integrity in every undertaking; faithful to his prince, and a lover of his country. An example worthy of imitation; and he was universally known and admired for his true spirit of patriotism, his death is greatly lamented."

Canon Chamberlain, in a paper read at Trinity College in 1946, mentions Prior's practical but effective style. "Molyneux might reason in high constitutional fashion against usurpation. Swift might lash out his fierce indignation against injustice. Prior might agree with both; but his practical mind concentrated on more immediate objectives. The distressed people needed, and needed at once, 'shoes to their feet, clothes to their backs and beef in their bellies' and Prior saw that, even within the existing evil framework of government policy, these pressing aims could be realised through voluntary self-help wisely directed and prudently assisted."

Clarke's thoroughly researched and well-written biography offers an excellent insight into Prior's life and principles: "Among his contemporaries, Prior stands out uniquely as one of the few who sought neither place, patronage nor honour. His friends, almost without exception, obtained lucrative preferments. That Prior could have held at least some

Memorial at Rathdowney Church.

of the minor offices in the patronage of Parliament cannot be doubted; instead he worked selflessly, content to spend his not too great fortune in the cause he espoused. He was not a wealthy man, yet the records of the Dublin Society clearly show that during his twenty years of secretary-ship, neither he nor indeed any of his colleagues, drew a single penny from the Society's funds, nor obtained any monetary advantage or bene-fit by reason of membership. Their work was voluntary, and the reward was the success they achieved."

Prior's importance in his own time and his aspirations to economic development and in improving social conditions many years ahead of his time are reflected in the contemporary and anonymously contributed satire, *A Dialogue between Dean Swift and Thomas Prior, Esq., in the Isles of St. Patrick's Church, Dublin, On that memorable Day, October 9th, 1753*. Swift is portrayed in a most pessimistic mood rejecting Prior's upbeat analysis of the Irish situation.[4]

Prior's death came as a bitter blow to the members of the Dublin Society. He had given twenty fruitful years to the Society and had been to the forefront in spearheading advances in all aspects of agriculture and industry as well as planning and helping to establish the School of Art. He was a patron of the arts in its many forms and it was appropriate that the impressive monument in his honour in Christchurch Cathedral was executed by the most famous sculptor then working in Ireland, Van Nost, "who from the earliest years of the Society was associated with its suc-cessful efforts to develop an Irish school of sculpture".[5] Van Nost had already sculpted for the Society busts of Prior and Madden and the bust which surmounts the monument which stands prominently in Christchurch south porch is a replica of the bust in the Society's posses-sion.

It was more appropriate still that Berkeley, the man who knew Prior best, should pen the obituary carved on the elegant marble monument as a lasting tribute to his dearest friend, "that worthy patriot to whom his own actions and unwearied endeavours in the service of his country have raised a monument more lasting than marble".

Berkeley's tribute was written, as Clarke expressed it, "in imperish-able Latin". The inscription reads:

Memoriae Sacrum
Thomas Prior;
Viri, siquis unquam alius, de patria
Optime meriti;
Qui, cum prodesse mallet quam conspici.

Prior Monument, Christchurch Cathedral (J. Van Nost).

Nec insenatum cooptatus
Nec consiliorum áulae particeps.
Nec ullo publico munere insignitus,
Rem tamen publicam
Mirisice auxit et ornavit
Auspiciis consiliis labore indesesso
Vir innocuus probus pius,
Partium studiis minime addictus,
De re familiari parum solicitus
Cum civium commoda unice spectaret.
Quicquid vel ad inopiae levamen,
Vel ad vitae elegantiam facit,
Quicquid ad desidiam populi vincendam,
Aut ad bonas artes excitandas pertinet,
Id omne pro virili excoluit;
Societatis Dubliniensis
Auctor, Institutor, Curator.
Quae fecerit
Pluribus dicere haud refert.
Quorsum narraret marmor
Illa quae civium animis insculpta
Nulla dies delebit.

The inscription has been translated as follows: "Sacred to the memory of Thomas Prior, a man deserving if ever there was one, the best regards of his country; who, preferring to be useful rather than to seem so, not elected to sit in Parliament, not chosen to be a member of the Privy Council, and not distinguished by any public office, nevertheless, wonderfully advanced and adorned the interests of the common weal by his guidance, counsels, and unwearied exertion. He was a man blameless, upright and religious; in no wise addicted to the interests of party; not too careful of his private fortune, since he took a singular interest in the benefits of his fellow citizens. Whatever conduced to the relief of poverty, or to the elegancies of life; whatever tended to overcome the want of enterprise of the people. and to the promotion of useful arts, that did he cultivate to the extent of his power. He was Promoter, Founder and Guardian of the Dublin Society. What he did need not, in further terms, be told. Why should marble relate what all men know. Those things namely, which are engraven on the hearts of his fellow citizens; and which no time can efface."

Prior's life was ended, but not his work. His lifetime of labour for the public good and his selfless dedication to promoting the aims and the ethos of the Society he founded inspired others to take up the torch he had lit and pass it on. The Society grew in size and influence and by the middle of the nineteenth century it wielded wide powers and prestige. It was subject only to Parliament and even in this respect it felt itself sufficiently secure and confident to challenge decisions of Government on occasions.

Though the RDS now is far from that of its exalted days at the epi-centre of Irish life, it still fulfils a significant role in modern day Ireland. Thomas Prior casts his shadow today, as he has done for the past two hundred and fifty years, on the Society he founded and, through its work, on Irish life. There were times during that quarter of a millennium when some members chose to act, and decisions were taken, in a manner which fell short of the highest principles exemplified by the founder. These were few, however, and were the exceptions to the general rule of high quality leadership and conduct which prevailed and which would have found Prior's approval. The prime status held by the Royal Dublin Society over the decades and centuries and its durability and capacity to adapt to the needs and challenges of the day stand testament to Prior, the doer, the ever-practical man, and to his work and achievements. The success story that is the RDS is the legacy of Thomas Prior.

References

(1) *Consumer Nationalism in 18th Century Dublin* by Sarah Foster (History Today, June 1997)
(2) Extract from a Letter from Sir Richard Cox to Thomas Prior Esq., *Showing from Experience a Sure Method to Establish Linen Manufactures and the Beneficial effect it will immediately produce.* 1749.
(3) *Berkeley's Bermuda Project* by A. A. Luce (Proceedings of the Royal Irish Academy, (Vol. XLII, Section C, No. 6). Dublin. 1934.
(4) See Appendix 5.
(5) From a note attributed to C. P. Curran by Clarke in his book, *Thomas Prior (1681-1751).*

Epilogue

The Dublin Society – which became known as the Royal Dublin Society when King George IV became patron on 29 June 1820 – was firmly established by the time of Prior's death in October 1751. The system of rewarding individuals and groups with premiums for experiments, inventions and initiatives which would benefit the economy and society flourished. These proved an encouragement to a wide range of projects, mainly agricultural or industrial related, but also acknowledged best practices and innovative ideas in almost every other aspect of human activity. By 1746, five years after the distribution of the first premiums, the list of grantees, covering such diverse projects as the collection of rags and waste material for paper manufacture to land drainage and reclamation extended to five written pages. Twenty years later the list of projects ran to twenty-six pages. Prior's enlistment of Samuel 'Premium' Madden to assist in the consolidation and growth of the Society had proven an inspired choice.

Prior had already secured some public funding through Lord Chesterfield's good offices in the form of a royal bounty of £500 a year. The Society's standing in official circles was further boosted by the granting of the Royal Charter in 1750 but it was not until 1761 that any substantial annual grant was made by the Irish Parliament. The Act which benefited the Society to the tune of £12,000 was a huge endorsement for the Society's incentive schemes. It specified that £10,000 was for distribution among petitioners for premiums and the remaining £2,000 was to be applied to increase premiums for agricultures and manufactures. Two years later £2,000 was specifically voted for agricultures and £7,000 for manufactures. The direct result of these grants was a big upsurge in activities undertaken by the Society.[1]

By this time the Society was already directly involved in a major commercial enterprise. In 1753 the guild of silk weavers in Dublin had presented a petition to Parliament claiming that their business was being ruined by imported silks. Parliament voted £3,200 to the Society to establish a silk warehouse for retail purposes. Premises were acquired in

Parliament Street, silk was sold and a commission paid to manufacturers. Prior, along with Berkeley, Swift, Dobbs, Molyneux, Molesworth and others, had all championed, for many years, the benefits of buying home produce, calling for the rejection of imported goods. The campaign against foreign imports grew in ferocity as the century progressed. The first organised protests by weavers took place in 1745, resulting in the imposition of heavy duties on French silks. Fashionable ladies became involved in the 'Buy Irish' campaign: "A Ladies Committee was formed to encourage manufactures under the presidency of Lady Townshend, the Lord Lieutenant's wife, the Duchess of Leinster, Lady Louisa Conolly, Lady Arabella Denny (a most charitable and public-spirited person) and other ladies of rank became patronesses."[2] Mrs. Delany notes in her writings that many ladies were dressed in Irish materials at a ball given by the viceroy, Lord Chesterfield, and that Lady Chesterfield appeared dressed from head to toe in Irish manufactures.

Trade restrictions on Irish goods to England and the colonies was an irksome issue that persisted well into the latter part of the eighteenth century. The campaign against foreign goods really took off during the economic downturn in the late 1770s which was exacerbated by urban depressions in Dublin and Cork. The woollen trade was in ruin and the linen industry was creaking under the punitive restrictions and duties imposed by the mother parliament at Westminster. A Protestant Volunteer corps, formed to protect property and suppress riots, became involved in the intensified campaign for "Free Trade" as Anglo-Irish relations deteriorated. As numbers in the Volunteers mushroomed, national self-confidence blossomed. Fearful of an Irish backlash, the British Government, under Lord North, duly delivered on easing trade restrictions but, by the early 1780s, there was a growing feeling that free trade could only be meaningful if it were controlled by an Irish parliament. Legislative independence was conceded in an act of 1782.

Because of pressure from various sources, the penal laws, which had been randomly and ever-decreasingly enforced, were eased by the British Government. The Catholic Relief Act of 1778 removed restrictions on Catholics holding long leases and four years later another act allowed them to buy or bequeath land in the same way as Protestants. The new opportunities allowed Catholics to engage in trade and soon they would become significant contributors to Ireland's economic growth. One wealthy Catholic merchant, John Keogh, boasted that the Dublin Society had awarded him their highest premium as the "greatest Purchaser of Irish silks in this Kingdom, by some Thousand Pounds".[3]

The Dublin Society handled substantial stocks of silk in their warehouse (an average of over £13,000) but despite their best efforts the trade continued to decline. Parliament directed the Society not to apply its funds towards the upkeep of the warehouse after 25 March, 1786. Meanwhile the Society opened a woollen warehouse in 1773 at Castle Street. Premiums were awarded to manufacturers. Woollen manufactures suffered an extreme depression in the early years of the nineteenth century. One of the Society's best supporters and renowned benefactor, Thomas Pleasants, erected a premises in the Liberties in Dublin at an expense of £12,964, to assist weavers in drying their goods. All to no avail, however, and eventually the Society ceded its interest in the warehouse.

These ventures into commercially driven activities stretched the resources of an organisation that had many other strings to its bow. It was agriculture and related activities, however, that were largely the bedrock of the Society from its foundation to almost the present day. Afforestation, tillage and land use generally, the reclamation of bog and scrubland all engaged the attention of the Society. Premiums or gold medals in lieu were given to those engaged in increasing production and improving their land and educational publications were sponsored. John Wynn Baker, an Englishman who settled in Ireland, purchased a farm near Celbridge and began a series of experiments in tillage and the planting of crops. His *Experiments in Agriculture* were published each year by the Society from 1764-70. At first Baker was grant-aided by the Society and later was paid an annual salary of £300. He made an important contribution to Irish agriculture but too much may have been expected from him with the limited funds made available to the project by the Society. Baker's cause was not helped by the growing influence of the industrial grouping within the Society who felt too much money was being invested in farming and too little in industry. Arthur Young (1741-1820), the renowned agricultural and travel writer of the period, knew and was impressed by Baker. He disapproved of what he perceived to be the Society's excessive role in industry, urging that it should get back to basics by concentrating its energy and resources on promoting agriculture. He was particularly critical of the low-level of funding made available by the Society to Baker's experiments. He also highlighted abuses in the system of premiums.

Botany, one of Prior's many preoccupations, was another of the Society's interests from its earliest days. Some of the other founder members too had a keen interest in, and a good knowledge of, the subject. Eighteen acres at Glasnevin were acquired in 1795 for the Botanic Gardens, which remain a major national attraction today. Gifts of plants

Great Exhibition of 1853.

from around the world were received and the directors travelled to the celebrated gardens in England, purchasing plants and arranging exchanges. Lectures were well attended and prizes and medals were awarded for examinations. The gardens declined for a time during the depression following the Napoleonic wars, leaving most of the buildings in ruins by 1830. This marked the lowest point in the gardens' history. In 1838 David Moore was elected Curator and he and his son, Sir Frederick Moore, between them gave almost 100 years of dedicated service in managing Ireland's major horticultural institution. The Government gave £4,000 and the Society added £1,000 for the erection of new greenhouses in 1843. Further grants were forthcoming and many improvements were made in the decades that followed. But the opening of the gardens to the public on Sundays was an issue which threatened the withdrawal of the Government grants. The Society regarded the gardens as a place for experiment and instruction rather than one of recreation. The move was also resisted on Sabbatharian grounds. The Government was, however, adamant that there be public accessibility to the gardens, even on Sundays, as was the case with London's Kew Gardens. In the face of mounting confrontation, the Society backed down. The Sunday opening experiment would prove to be hugely successful.

From the opening years of the nineteenth century, the Dublin Society promoted the idea of a veterinary college. But it was not until 1895 that it succeeded in its aim. The Royal Veterinary College of Ireland was established under charter that year and of the twenty members on the governing body, twelve were to be provided by the Society. Control of the College was transferred to the Irish Department of Agriculture and Technical Instruction in 1913. The Department relinquished its teaching role in 1960 and two university schools of veterinary medicine were established at the National University and Trinity College.

The arts, too, have always been central to the Society's activities. Premiums played an important part in the promotion of drawing, painting and sculpture for more than a century and prospered under its wing. Prior, no doubt, had ensured that the promotion of the "useful arts" was enshrined in the Society's constitution and it was he who first floated the idea of setting up an academy or drawing school. He solicited, and duly received, Chesterfield's approval of his plan in 1746 during the latter's brief tenure as Lord Lieutenant. Madden's premiums for the best drawings by boys and girls under the age of sixteen prompted the establishment of the school. Pupils' drawings were exhibited annually in a room in the Irish House of Lords at College Green. As activities expanded, more space was needed. In 1758 the stables at Shaw's Court were converted for use by the drawing school and also for the keeping of sculpted pieces. Ten years later the school moved to premises in Grafton Street and in 1796 it was relocated in the Society's premises in Abbey Street and Hawkins Street. Leinster House was acquired by the Society in 1815, making it possible to exhibit its growing collections of sculptures and paintings and to house the art school and the library. The Society continued to manage the school until 1877 when responsibilities were taken over by the government Department of Science and Art. The school became the Metropolitan School of Art and the sculptures, casts, prints, drawings and models were handed over to that body.

The RDS has, for the past century and a half, facilitated the mounting of major exhibitions of every kind and still does so today. The first exhibition of Irish manufactures took place in 1833. By 1853 the biggest exhibition of the century was being held on the Society's premises at Leinster Lawn. It was sponsored to the tune of £40,000 by William Dargan, the railway builder and enterpreneur extraordinaire. By the time the show was over, Dargan was said to have advanced £100,000, having lost a considerable amount of that in the process: "The authorities conflict as to whether Dargan lost £20,000 … and refused a Baronetcy, or £10,000 and refused a Knighthood."[4] It seems certain Dargan could have received a royal honour had he so desired. Quite similar to his fellow Queen's County man of a hundred years earlier, however, the public good meant more to him than public acclaim. Queen Victoria attended the Exhibition and was so impressed by what she saw that after her visit to Leinster Lawn, she drove out to see Dargan and his wife at their home at Mount Anville House, Dundrum.

The interest created by the exhibition of industries, antiquities and fine arts led to the foundation of the National Gallery of Ireland. Dargan once again contributed funds, this time £5,000 to promote the founding of the Gallery. Some 346 drawings owned by the Society were transferred there and many prominent RDS members made gifts of paintings. To this day the President and Vice-President of the Society are ex-officio members of the Board of Governors and Guardians of the Gallery. The Society commissioned a bronze statue of Dargan, who was born in County Laois, just across from the River Barrow at Carlow, and the life-size cast now stands, fittingly, at the front of the National Gallery buildings at Leinster Lawn. On the opposite side of Leinster Lawn, the foundation stone for the Natural History Museum had been laid on 7 March 1856, with most of the collections having been moved there by 1862. Ownership of these buildings and collections were transferred to the state in 1877.

Neither was scientific advancement neglected by the Society. Between 1787 and 1792, the Leskean mineral collection, the Society's most significant acquisition of its kind, which was formed in Germany and comprised of 7,331 mineral specimens, was purchased on its behalf by Dr. Richard Kirwan, appointed Professor of Mineralogy to the Society in 1792. A survey of the Leinster coalfields on behalf of the Society was carried out by Richard Griffith, of Griffith's Valuation fame, in 1809 and three years later he was appointed Mining Engineer and Professor of Geology to the Society. A museum of economic geology was opened at 51 St. Stephen's Green and Sir Robert Kane, the Society's lecturer in natural philosophy, was appointed its first director. The title was changed to the Museum of Irish Industry in 1852 and on the government undertaking full support of the institution in 1867 its title became the Royal College of Science. A new building was erected to house the College in 1911 and it was later absorbed by University College, Dublin.

From the second half of the eighteenth century, the Society, through benefactions from its members, developed collections of antiques and exquisite artefacts from around the world as well as rare and precious items from Ireland's own past. A collection of over 1,300 objects was transferred to the National Museum which was established under the Dublin Science and Art Museum Act of 1877. The National Library was founded under the same act. Both buildings face each other at the south and north sides respectively of the courtyard entrance to Leinster House. The Dublin Society began its library collection in its very first year of existence and this expanded rapidly, helped greatly by the gift of Dr. Jasper Joly who presented 23,000 volumes in 1863. It had acquired an estimated 100,000 volumes by the time of the transfer of most of the collection to the state in 1890. The Society retained about 10,000 volumes which would become the basis for the present library at Ballsbridge.

The Dublin Society, through its members and its innovations, played a central role in the golden age of Irish architecture. The most striking physical reminders today of the era of enlightenment are to be seen in the wonderful architectural heritage of 18th century Dublin. Trinity College, Tailor's Guild Hall, Dr. Steevan's Hospital and Dublin Castle all date from the early 1700s. Names associated with the Society and its activities include the aforementioned Richard Cassells, whose landmarks include Leinster House, Newman House and Batholomew Mosse's Rotunda Hospital, and James Gandon, whose creations include some of the great civic buildings of the city, the Custom House, The Four Courts and The King's Inns. The Society's positive influence extended to the

The Horse Show of 1923 with the Masonic School in the background. The RDS purchased the school in the 1970s and re-named it Prior House. The Society subsequently disposed of the property which is now converted into a hotel.

Wide Street Commission under whose guidance the graceful Georgian thoroughfares, such as Merrion and Fitzwilliam Squares, Mount and Henrietta Streets and Beresford Place came into being. In 1758 Thomas Ivory, one of the most respected architects of the day, was appointed to teach architectural drawing at Shaw's Court and for many generations into the future, the Dublin Society continued to give the lead in architectural training and design not only in the Irish context but also to London itself. Edward McParland, the architectural historian, has implied that the public building programme of the eighteenth century Ireland was influenced by two forces: a desire to do things bigger and better than London, and to by-pass London by looking to other foreign sources, particularly France.

The issue of Sunday opening at the Botanic Gardens was not the only instance of conflict between the Dublin Society and the Government. The Society could not function without the state grants while the Government had to ensure that it was money well spent. There was constant tension between the two until the Society became more or less financially self-dependent, having divested itself of the responsibilities of running the major institutions when they were transferred to the state towards the end of the nineteenth century.

Although the Society was non-political, it was impossible to divorce happenings in the country and in the outside world from the thinking within. The 1798 rebellion and the ensuing Act of Union had roused fears and passions among Society members, invariably Anglo-Irish and Protestant. The ascendancy positively felt the earth shifting beneath their feet with the growing public pressure and parliamentary support for Catholic emancipation. The Bill giving Catholics the right to hold senior public office and sit in Parliament was passed by the House of Commons as early as 1821 but it received a hostile reception in the House of Lords. The spectacular victory of Daniel O'Connell in the 1828 by-election in Co. Clare led to the final push which convinced the ruling Tories that emancipation could not be delayed any longer. The last Catholic Relief Act (Catholic Emancipation) became law on 13 April 1829. Anglo-Irish fears of losing their privileges were further heightened with the passing of the Reform Act of 1832 which allowed large towns the right to share political power with the landlords.

It was against this background that the Dublin Society (by then the Royal Dublin Society) came in major conflict with the Government. At the Society's weekly meeting on Thursday, 26 November, 1835, the Catholic Archbishop of Dublin, Dr. Daniel Murray, was one of several candidates nominated for membership. A mild-mannered scholar, he was backed by some influential members. But it was a step too far for many other members and the unusually large attendance gave the good Archbishop the thumbs down. He was blackballed – just as Daniel O'Connell had been twenty-three years earlier. If members could justify their snubbing of O'Connell, outspoken and highly political, it was infinitely harder to find a valid reason, short of sectarianism, for rejecting the Archbishop's application. The Government was alarmed. Though the Archbishop was first to admit that the Society had the right to do what they did, this did not put an end to the matter. The row over grants and the way the Society conducted its business waged on for years until the issue was overshadowed by other events, especially by the devastation of the Great Famine.

Acquiring the land at Ballsbridge in the late nineteenth century proved a very wise move with the shows and activities housed there soon enabling the Society to pay its own way and not having to depend upon Government bailouts. The British Army took up occupation of Ballsbridge during the course of World War One and troops based there were involved in crushing the 1916 Rising. Politics again reared its ugly head when the Council's recommendation that George Noble Count Plunkett be called upon to resign from membership on the grounds that after the Rising he had been arrested, deported and dismissed from the post of Director of the National Museum. As father of Joseph Mary Plunkett, who was executed after the Rising, he inevitably faced the wrath of the ascendancy dominated Society: "The great majority of the traditional membership in 1917 must be presumed to have been staunch adherents to the British connection. They cannot possibly have liked what they saw around them after 1916 … Most certainly it was not the happiest way for the Society to greet the emerging new Ireland."[5]

The newly independent Dáil Éireann obtained a portion of Leinster House in 1922 for parliamentary use and two years later took possession of the entire building. Leinster House remains today the seat of Irish Government. The Society transferred its headquarters to Ballsbridge in November 1924. Despite the seismic change in the political order, it showed a *Realpolitik* approach in quickly adjusting to the new political environment. It continued to play a key role in the New Ireland as it had in the Old. Another military occupation followed, this time by the Irish Army for the duration of World War Two. Even during those dark days the Society, in the face of adversity as so often in the past, showed its remarkable resilience; a resilience which has carried it from strength to strength into the third millennium.

In the final years of the eighteenth century the Society, backed by grants from the Irish Parliament, embarked on a mission to investigate the overall state of Irish agriculture, on which there was a lack of information. Detailed studies were required. A county-by-county agricultural survey had already been carried out in Scotland and England and these models were used for the Irish project. Almost on the eve of its dissolution in the year 1800, Parliament passed an act granting the Society £15,000, of which a part was to be used to finance a survey. Laois was selected as the first county under the study. This document *General View of Agriculture and Manufactures of the Queen's County with Observations on the Means of their Improvement* by Sir Charles Coote was published in 1801. By the end of the following year, fifteen surveys had been issued but now the ill consequences of the Union were beginning to take effect and the Society had to contend with reduced grants which slowed down the progress of the surveys and on other fronts. In all, twenty three surveys were published which give us a pretty accurate and comprehensive account of the state of agriculture for the period.

Though improving the breeds of livestock was a relatively minor activity for the Society in its early years the momentum generated by local farming societies – which were being established countrywide in the late eighteenth century – culminated in the year 1800 in the foundation of the Farming Society of Ireland 'under the patronage of the Dublin Society'. This group undertook most of the agricultural activities of the parent body and, according to Meenan and Clarke, "must be credited with the first serious effort to improve Irish livestock".[6]

The Farming Society received an annual grant of £5,000 from the Government, exactly half the grant that the parent body was then receiving. The Dublin Society shed most of its commitments to agriculture but still helped the new society with grants, the publication of information on agriculture and experiments at the Botanic Gardens. A fall in agricultural exports signalled the start of a decline in the Farming Society and the Government grant ceased in 1828. In 1841 the Agricultural Improvement Society was established with the backing of the Royal Dublin Society. The support of farming organisations around the country was sought to enable the new body function as a replacement for the Farming Society.

The first livestock show took place in the yard adjoining Leinster House in April 1831. The numbers of animals entered and their quality of improved in the years that followed. The annual Spring Show had arrived. Expanding to encompass farm machinery and implements from 1851, the Show was transferred from Kildare Street to Ballsbridge thirty years later. In 1924 it developed into a general trade show remaining the biggest annual agricultural event in Ireland until 1992 when it was outflanked by the National Ploughing Championships which replaced it as the major farming event of the year.

With the demise of the Spring Show, there was no recognised national event where the best of Irish livestock could be judged and exhibited, thus leaving a clear national void. The RDS addressed the problem in the year 2000 by reviving the Spring Show livestock classes. Goffs Bloodstock Sales on the Naas Road was chosen as the venue because of its convenient location. There was an enthusiastic response from breeders and the public to the Show, auguring well for the re-emergence of the RDS as a neutral but well informed part of the Irish livestock industry into the future.

A similarly celebrated event, the Horse Show, was first organised jointly by the Agricultural Improvement and Royal Dublin Societies in 1864 and again in 1866. The following year the RDS Committee of Agriculture decided that it should become an annual event and the first Show akin to its present format was held in 1868. It grew in popularity and, like the Spring Show, found a new home in Ballsbridge in 1881. Within a decade it had become an international tourist attraction and a top social event. The introduction of international showjumping in 1926 sparked a new era of growth. Record crowds saw the Switzerland team win the first competition for the Aga Khan Cup.

Today the Horse Show remains the highest profile event on the RDS calendar. Now sponsored by Kerrygold, Ballsbridge houses not only one of the longest established but also one of the top horse shows, sharing with Aachen in Germany and Calgary in Canada a place in the top major events of its kind in the world. The Horse Show is an integral part of Dublin and Irish tradition, a unique event that combines high international standing and reputation with strong historical connotations and pageantry. It also provides a shop-window for the non-thoroughbred, an important part of the horse industry which is a significant element in the Irish economy. The exhibition of category winners in the RDS Crafts Competition is now an integral part of annual Horse Show programme.

The RDS today, as it has done since its foundation, has a useful role to play in Irish life, reacting to the needs of the day, especially those related to farming. The Society, through its Agriculture and Rural Development Committee, runs and administers the leading farm environmental award in the country, the Profitable Farm and Conservation Award Scheme. There is also a special award scheme for the promotion of good forestry practice. Another innovation has been introduced by the Equestrian Committee which involves educating urban children about the care of horses. There is also a project to increase the awareness among such children of the realities of food production and farm life.

From a public perspective, the RDS is today well known as the most important exhibition centre in the country. Scarcely a week goes by in which the RDS is not host to some major exhibition. Agricultural bodies use its facilities as does every other sector of society. The premises at Ballsbridge is also well-known as a live entertainment centre, a venue which can cater for mass audiences.

The proud tradition of talented people devoting their time and energy on a voluntary basis in promoting the Society's aims and activities continues today. The voluntary effort is backed by a highly competent and dedicated executive staff which ensures that the oldest society of its kind in the world is as vibrant as it has ever been.

The full history of the Royal Dublin Society is well recorded elsewhere as is the contribution of the members and officers responsible for maintaining its unique record of achievement in so many fields of activity over so many years for the benefit of the nation and its people. The creation of this worthy institution was once a dream and the purpose of this book is to acknowledge the man who turned the dream into reality. As de Vere White commented: "I find it difficult to believe that without him … the Royal Dublin Society would ever have been called into being."

References

(1) *The Royal Dublin Society 1731-1981* edited by James Meenan and Desmond Clarke. Dublin. 1981.

(2) *The Story of the Royal Dublin Society* by Terence de Vere White. Tralee. 1956.

(3) *Consumer nationalism in 18th-century Dublin* by Sarah Foster. Article published in the magazine, History Today, June 1997.

(4) As (2).

(5) As (1).

(6) As (1).

Notes on ancestry and family of Thomas Prior

The subject of this book's name appears in bold print.

(1) Robert Prior (great grandfather of **Thomas Prior**) b: 1576 in Cambridge; d: 1644

(2) His son: Captain Thomas Prior (grandfather of **Thomas Prior**) came to Ireland with his regiment in 1636; died (March 17) 1691

(3) Captain Thomas Prior's family: Colonel Thomas (father of **Thomas Prior**) d: 1700 (killed by rebels); Richard (uncle) d. 1726 at Ely, Cambridge; Mary (aunt) married Rev. Thomas Murray.

(4) Colonel Thomas Prior's family: Richard (brother) b: 1677 (noted by O'Hanlon as Co. Magistrate for Queen's County in 1714) ; Isabella (sister) b: 1678; Ann (sister) b: 1680; **Thomas b: 1681; d: 21 October 1751**; Elizabeth (sister) b: 1682 and half brothers Robert and William.

Clarke, during the course of his research on his book on Thomas Prior in 1951, received a letter, now in the R.D.S. archives, from a Mr. E. C. Prior with an address in Long Island, New York, giving some unverified information ("the story as I often heard it when a boy") on **Thomas Prior's** father and his brothers: "When his (Colonel Thomas Prior) first wife died, he married the daughter of a small farmer who was remarkably good looking. The marriage was kept secret, how I don't know, and particularly so from his own children. The elder son having died (first wife) and **Thomas** being a bachelor with no intentions of getting married, it had been talked of between the members of the family (probably excluding the Colonel) that young Mr. Murray would succeed to the property." The letter also tells us that "Colonel Thomas Prior ... was a rollicking-going, breezy individual as can be readily recognised from the facts available on record as well as from what was known and carried down in the family." I failed to uncover "the facts available on record" and so cannot verify this account of the Colonel's exuberant attributes.

The letter also asserts that "Robert Prior was a good man and that it was his son, John, who, in particular, was 'no good' and later, of course, William eclipsed them all". The writer also advised Clarke that he did not know of any Richard Prior ... "as having been disinherited".

Clarke states that Prior left his estate to John Murray, son of his Aunt Mary, who was married to Rev. Thomas Murray. John Murray later adopted the name of Prior. The young Mr. Murray referred to in the letter to Clarke from Mr. E.C. Prior in the U.S. in 1951 referred to above seems most likely to be John Murray Prior, son of **Thomas Prior's** Aunt Mary. His Aunt Mary may have been the child of a second marriage of an ageing Captain Prior, who died in 1691, if she was still of child-bearing age circa 1720, when John was born. John is clearly shown as the first named of his cousins in Thomas Prior's (the subject's) will.

The General Armory of England, Scotland, Ireland and Wales confirms that John Murray was, indeed, a son of Prior's Aunt Mary. "Prior (Roding, Co. Essex, subsequently settled in the counties of Oxford, Lancaster and Cambridge; a descendant of the family, **Thomas Prior**, Esq. of Rathdowney, Queen's County, the celebrated founder of the RDS d. in 1751, having devised his property to his cousin, John Murray, only son of the Rev. Thomas Murray by Mary, his wife, daughter of Captain Thomas Prior, the first settler in Ireland.)

MacLysaght in a letter to Clarke on 9 March 1951 referred to an abstract (not a copy) of Thomas Prior's will ("at the Castle") dated 22 June 1751 (four months before his death): "**Thomas Prior**, testator, unmarried, one brother, Robert, unm.; cousins John Murray, Sarah Archdall, wife of James Morris, Thomas, son of William Fitzgerald, Isabella, wife of Barry Coller, Susanna Meredith."

Rathdowney in south-east Queensland was named by Thomas Lodge Murray-Prior, a large freeholder in the district, in 1876. He was a direct descendant of John Murray Prior. He was born Nov. 13, 1819 in Wessl, Somerset and died Dec. 18, 1892 in Maroon (Logan River, Queensland). He emigrated to Australia in 1839. A descendant of his, Thomas A. Murray-Prior, from New South Wales visited the RDS and met the President, Col. W. A. Ringrose in 1999.

O'Hanlon's *History of the Queen's County* (Appendix 1V) notes that Richard Prior was a County Magistrate in 1714 – (with reference to Hanaper and the Records Office, Dublin). It also notes that a **Thomas Prior** held a similar position in 1738 as did John Murray Prior in 1753. O'Hanlon notes too that a Thomas Prior was County Sheriff in 1799.

APPENDIX 2

Rathdowney

This is Carrigan's account of Rathdowney in his History of the Diocese of Ossory (1905).

"Irish speakers in the Co.Kilkenny always call it Raw-dhouna, i.e. Rath Domhnaigh, the Rath of the Domhnach or Church; and this, too, is the form of the name found in the *Three Fragments of Annals*. The *Four Masters*, on the other hand, write the name Rath Tamhnaigh (pronounced Raw-thaouna), which signifies the Rath of Tamhnach, i.e. of the green meadow-field.

The "Rath" from which the nme has its origin, was situated at the north side of Rathdowney Square, in which Mr. Patrick Murphy's yard and garden, 159 yards north-east of the Protestant church. It was circular in shape, 25 or 30 yards in diameter nd flat at the top, and raised about 8 ft. over the surrounding land. John Howard, of The Garrison, Rathdowney, who levelled the rath, about 1840, informed the writer that he found it filled with human bones (but there were no skulls), and that he removed five cart-load of them thence for interment elsewhere; that there were no traces of foundations or walls, nor headstones, and that if any such were there, they were removed before he could remember, the rath having been used as a cabbage garden even before he was born; and that he found there some bone pins 2 or 2.5 inches long, but no objects of iron or bronze, or anything else of interest. The presence of such a great quantity of human bones would certainly point to the rath as the site of n ancient churchyard, and, consequently, of a Domhnach or Church.

Carrigan also notes: "as a town, Rathdowney cannot boast of any great antiquity. It must have been a very small village in 1665, as only about a dozen persons pai hearth-money in the whole townland of Rathdowney in this year. Even since 1820 the town has been considerably enlarged.

The Garrison House

Prior's birthplace, The Garrison House, Rathdowney, was given its name for the obvious reason that it was the hub of the military and judicial presence for the area. In his "History of the Queen's County" O'Hanlon recounts a incident from penal times when there was a price on the head of a priest. A priest was shot dead, probably before 1700 "at a Mass-station in Pat Conroy's field on Knockeel hill. His murderers cut off his head and carried it in triumph to the Garrison in Rathdowney, where they received the usual reward, £5. For this and other like services to the State they and their descendants were long afterwards known by the sobriquet, na gceann, i.e., of the Heads."

A century later the Garrison was central to another swift dispensation of justice. This account is taken from "Parish of Borris-in-Ossory" by Brother Walsh : "A grave still pointed out in Rathdowney Square, the origin of which has puzzled the local inhabitants for many yers, dates from this period. It is known locally as the 'Croppy's grave', and has always been treated with respect and reverence. In 1798, Jerome Watson, a native of Crosspatrick, parish of Johnstown, was tried in the Garrison, Rathdowney, for an attempted robbery of firearms from the house of Mr. Vicars of Leevally, on 17th March, during which attempt the steward, Mr. Whitaker, was accidentally shot dead. William Vicars, writing to his brother Thomas in Dublin on 21st March, confirmed the murder of Whitaker, adding that some of the windows in the house were broken, and that he himself was obliged to seek refuge, every night since, at the residence of Robert Flood of Middlemount. A servant girl who was injured in the affray gave evidence for the prosecution, and swore that Watson and a man named Hennessy from Moore St., Rathdowney, were guilty of the murder of Whitaker. Hennessy escaped from the district and was never heard of again. Following his conviction Watson was flogged by a man named Harney under the orders of Robert Flood, J.P., Middlemount, Commander of the Ossory Cavalry, who was primarily responsible for the execution. Watson was then placed on a cart, and hanged from a tree in Rathdowney Square, the rope having been tied around his neck by a young son of Dr. Jacob of Knockfinn. The cart was then drawn from under him, the body cut down, and buried in a grave already prepared for it beneath the tree. A can of lime was thrown over the body by Walter Phelan of Ballycoolid, and the grave was then closed. An oblong patch of ground covered with gravel now marks the grave in which Watson was interred."

As an addendum to the account of that execution in 1798 in his unpublished pamphlet, "Outline History and Gleanings of Rathdowney-Errill Parish", dated 1975, a copy of which is held in Laois County Library, local historian, Andy Dowling, retells the incident and notes, "The Grim tale is well supported by the visible outline of the unforunate man's grave beneath the lime trees that grace the square. It is to the credit of the Co. Council or perhaps the local overseer, that in the resurfacing with tarmacadam the paved grave wasn't interfered with or covered up, because even as a curiosity it evokes a prayer and a thought in the minds of men".

The Battle of Borris-in-Ossory

Extract from: *Some Account of the Ruinous Ecclesiastical Edifices, Forts, Castles, &c., with notes of Modern Events connected with the Queen's County and County of Kildare* by M. C. Carey (Maryborough, 1901).

Carey quotes a Government report of the battle at Borris-in-Ossory in 1642: "… the garrison of Athy and Maryborough with the assistance of Captain George Greames made out 400 foot and 80 horse for the relief of Borris-in-Ossory, a castle belonging to the Duke of Buckingham in which were several English in great distress. It was no sooner resolved on than two soldiers of the county fled and gave the enemy notice of our coming. The Lord of Upper Ossory prepared to give resistance with about 800 foot and 60 or 80 horse, and on a 'straight' on a bog side set on our men. They received them with great resolution, and four of Greame's troops charged and routed them with the assistance of musketeers who were sent to clear the passage; yet they stood again and our foot killed 80 of theirs. Their horses retreated further off, and on the bog side made a stand, which being prepared by Cornet Wilbrow (Cornet to Sir Adam Loftus) he rode up to them and charged them home. They had the bog at their back; our horse so bestirred themselves, they slew 40 of their best freeholders; among them was the brother of the Lord of Upper Ossory who was slain, and Florence Fitzpatrick they say is desperately wounded. The names of the chief rebels slain were – Dermot MacTeague Fitzpatrick, uncle of the Lord of Upper Ossory; Dermot Óger, his son; Captain Layer, a low country soldier; Burke, his Lieutenant; Captain Dermot MacAboy; Patrick Cashion of the Cross; Bryan Connor, heir to Patrick Connor; Captain John Cashin, Gentleman; Morgan Cashin; William O'Carroll, a chief freeholder; Donogh Fitzpatrick, Gentleman;a son of Bryan MacWilliam, Loughlin Costigan; Patrick Costigan; Friar John Costigan; Patrick Hoare, a priest; Mat Delaney, a sub-sheriff; John Tobin, a merchant of Kilkenny; Sergeant Bryan Burke &c., besides Lieurenant O'More, prisoner at Burras." Carey adds: "At a place called Glais-na-Muck on the Nore near Borris some years ago, were found several old arms and pieces opf swords and bayonets. It is not improbable that this was the site alluded to."

A Dialogue between Dean Swift and Thomas Prior

Extracts from *A Dialogue between Dean Swift and Thomas Prior Esq., on the Isles of St. Patrick's Church, Dublin, On that memorable day, October 9th, 1753*, attributed to "A friend to the Peace and Prosperity of Ireland" and printed for G and A Ewing at the Angel and Bible in Dame Street in 1753.

The dialogue between the old friends, awakened from the dead, opens with concerns expressed for the troubled state of the country.

Prior: *Mr. Dean, I am sorry to see you up, if any of your private affairs disturb you. I came to call at your Grave, and have a little discourse with you ...*

Swift: *'Tis my country keeps me walking! Why who can be still? I dont believe there are many Ghosts now, that have any share of Understanding, or any regard for Ireland, that are to be found in their Graves at Midnight. For my part I can no more keep in my Den than if it were the Day of Judgment. I have been earthed now eight years last October, and I think on my Conscience (and you know Tom the Conscience of one dead Man is worth ten of those that are living) I have had very few good Days Sleep since I got there. Ah Tom! poor Ireland! poor Ireland! It plagued my heart while I was trifling away life there, but my curse on it, I never thought it would have broke my heart thus when I was dead. I have tumbled and tossed from one side to the other (and by the by, they make these cursed coffins so narrow 'tis a plague to be in them) first one thing would come into my head, and then another, and often wrought me so, that I have many a time been forced to walk a whole Moon to rest me and get the better Nap when I lay down. Prithee how have you done? ... What makes you sigh so, Tom?*

Prior: *... I am chiefly grieved at the ill Circumstances of Ireland. My next trouble is, that the World seems resolved they shall never mend; and, I think so, by their treating all true patriots in the most unhandsome Manner. This is as mad a Measure, as imprisoning the Physicians in an epidemical sickness would be. Yet such Men, who only could heal our distempers, are treated almost as common Poisoners, and watched as if they were incendiaries and the Enemies of Society. It was too much our own Case when we were among Men and tho' I scorn to lament the indifferent Treatment Dean Swift and Tom Prior received from those who should have respected and honoured them; yet I cannot help being concerned for the hard Usage all true Patriots generally meet with in Ireland ... Let those whose Miserable Aim is writing well, be ashamed if they are criticis'd, or ridiculed, but he who sincerely strives to serve Millions must have a scorn for Malice or Satyr, if he thinks he can feed or cloath half a Nation by scribbling. I profess I writ whatever I published, barely for the Joy I had in doing some Service to my Country, and with so little a view to Reputation that I have done it if there had been no such thing as fame in the World ... Hence it was that I troubled the World with a deal of Tracts and publick Subjects; and I thank Heaven, my heart is a little ashamed of it, now I am dead, as I was proud of it when I was living, which is what few Authors can say when they are coffined. I saw writing absolutely necessary to the well-being of the most neglected Nation under Heaven ...*

(A discourse followed on those – and there were many – who vehemently criticised Swift. The Dean responds.)

Swift: *Dear Tom, they never gave me a moment's pain, for the Truth is, I was too proud to be offended, and had too high a Spirit to be humbled by such Insults. Many of their Tracts were the poorest Productions that ever disgraced the Press; without Style, or Wit or Sense or Argument.*

(Prior then mentions Swift's failure to attain higher office in the Church, a subject which grates the Dean's sensitivities.)

Swift: *I renounce it! I deny it! I lost nothing by not being preferred, but an enlarged Power of doing Good; and the day is coming (and sooner than the Feeders on the Earth imagine) when I shall be allowed as fully, for the good I would have done as for that which I was able to accomplish ... I saw in this same scurvy World, so many bad Men pass for Good; so many Fools pass for Wise; so many Ignorants for*

Learned; and so many Knaves for Honest, and rewarded accordingly; that I was rather provok'd than mortified! ... For all that Tom, tho' a Man hates Lyons and Tygers, there is no great Wit or Wisdom in throwing Stones at them, and provoking the lordly Monsters, to try the strength of their Mouths or their Fangs on you.

(The dialogue drifts into a debate and comments on the state of the country. Swift opens up on the state of the roads.)

Swift: *Ah Tom, I know very well, if Ireland had almost as many highWays in it as the Ocean, what advantages it would produce to us. This was one of the great Arts of the ancient Romans, who had prodigious Roads running through every Province, in a strait Line to the Capital of the Empire.*

(Prior then talks on "our prodigious number of converts and Charter schools ... and that soon Conformists, Dissenters and Papist will live in harmony together". Swift warns him about the Dissenters and the converts, especially "when their Conversion is brought about by worldly interests and securing their Estates". The discussion turns to population and poverty.)

Swift: *If, as political writers agree, the true Interests of any Country consists in the Prosperity not of Some, but of all the People in it, then I am sure Ireland, with her boasted numbers is in a bad way; as all her Popish Natives, or in other words three-fourths of her swarming Inhabitants, have neither Houses, Cloaths, Work, Food, or Fire. This is a dismal self-evident Truth that demands consideration ... at the same time our Nobility and Gentry set their lands excessively high, get their rents paid to the penny, have as little fear of Wars or Taxes as of Famines, and live as well (rambling and squandering their fortune all over the World) as any people whatever; without one uneasy thought as to the circumstances of those Crowds of their countrymen that are starving at home.*

(Next the discussion turns to the linen industry, so strongly promoted by Prior in his lifetime and this leads onto the work of the Dublin Society. Prior's talk on improvements are refuted one by one by the Dean.)

Prior: *Hear me out ... for I am so far from having done, that I have not yet touched on all the Advantages that our country has received, from the Dublin Society's Premiums; which was one of my chief reasons, for having considered Ireland as open to recovery, when I went underground like a Tortoise, to be raised again when the Summer comes, after a long sleep ... They gave Premiums to heighten the manufacture* *and Dyeing of our Woollen Cloths; of our Silks, and our Velvets; of our Blankets, of our Worsteds; of our Cotton, of our Cossap, Bulbs, Lutherines and Fustians; of our Stockings, and our Carpets, with surprising success. In our Husbandry they did Wonders also; as to Wheat and Barley; as to Liming, Marling, and Sanding of Land, as to planting Hops, draining of Bogs; as to raising Liquorise, Saffron and Madder; as to sowing of Turnips, Clover, St. Foil, Trefoil and all kinds of Grass seeds. They improved by a well judged Emulation and Proper Rewards, Numbers of our Husbandry utensils; They set the Nation at Work, in Planting amazing Quantities of Timber Trees, Willows and Osiers for Hop Poles; in raising great numbers of Orchards, and improving our making of Cyder, home made Wines, and Metheglins; as also in Brewing our Ale and Beer, and giving us vinegar from our own fruits, equal to the best in France. They raised the manufacture of our finest Hats, to a surprising degree; and they did the same by our Window Grass and made so great a progress in our Paper Business and Building of Mills for carrying it on, as if they got the mines of Peru, or the Industry of China, to assist them in their undertakings.*

(Prior is only halfway through his list of improvements helped by the Dublin Society's incentive schemes. Swift is getting bored. He asks Prior what he would do to improve the lot of the poor if he were still alive. Prior talks of the potential of the Dublin Society, of increased participation and sponsorship to promote virtues and good culture in the people. Various other issues are discussed. Prior looks on the optimistic side but Swift remains unimpressed.)

Swift: *... Dreams! Whims! And Delusions! If you had wrote yourself as blind as Milton did, what service could you do a nation that never thinks. You might as well expect to cure the Deaf by talking to them; idiots by reasoning with them; or to raise the Dead as the Romans did by bawling and weeping for their miserable conditions ...*

Prior: *Dear Dean, you are too severe and have too embittered a way of speaking on all things relating to Ireland.*

(Swift concludes on a depressed note and with a wake-up call for the Government.)

Swift: *Dear Tom, most men scarce begin to think till they're summoned to die and that I fear must be the case of Ireland, unless the Parliament helps us ...*

Index